Also by Adel Bishtawi

Fiction

Time of Death and Roses (*A novel*)
Traces of a Tattoo (*A novel*)
Gardens of Despair (*A novel*)
Don't Kill the Canary (*Short stories*)
The Lover (*Short stories*)
The Colour of Perfume (*A novella and short stories*)

Other Genres

Natural Foundations of Arab Civilisation
Origin of the Arabic Numerals
Martyrdom of the Andalusian Nation
The Andalusian Moriscos
History of Injustice in the Arab World
Manifest Destiny of Imperial Decline
The Greatest Gods of Homo Sapiens

Selvi Sado

The co-author of this book Selvi Agim Sado experimented with poetry at a very early stage, was and will be, an avid reader of poetry and an excellent judge of poetic qualities. Without her dedication, encouragement and inspiration this collection may not have been compiled and published. Selvi commands three languages: her native Albanian, French and English. She studied at the Faculty of Foreign Languages, University of Tirana, Albania.

ONLY WHEN DESIRE
SCREAMS

And other poems

ADEL BISHTAWI & SELVI SADO

author**HOUSE**®

AuthorHouse™ UK
1663 Liberty Drive
Bloomington, IN 47403 USA
www.authorhouse.co.uk
Phone: UK TFN: 0800 0148641 (Toll Free inside the UK)
          UK Local: (02) 0369 56322 (+44 20 3695 6322 from outside the UK)

Published by AuthorHouse 10/17/2022

ISBN: 978-1-7283-7598-4 (sc)
ISBN: 978-1-7283-7600-4 (hc)
ISBN: 978-1-7283-7599-1 (e)

Dedications

For all of you

When all is heard and all is told,
And all is read and all is said,
And not much there is to add,
Forget those who wronged you,
And with a happy heart remember,
All those who made you glad,
With whom the heart was paired,
By those who really cared,
Time is lost when lonely,
Time gained when time is shared,
They are parts of every wonder,
And the sum of all the parts,
The music made in heaven is played,
By the strings of loving hearts.
    Adel

To mum and dad,

Thank you for the love, dedication and care you generously gave a loving daughter who will always be proud of you; to my forever Gentian: THANK YOU FOR EVERYTHING.
    Selvi

CONTENTS

Only When Desire Screams..1

I Heard It Told 2

Young Love...3

Share A Child 4

Pregnant 5

For You And For Me...6

I Am Woman,...7

New Equilibrium..8

Family 9

Just Say "Sorry"...10

I See Desire In Your Eyes 11

Life Is Great..12

Go To Hell..13

Hand In Hand 14

Breathless 15

Who Wants To Be A God? 16

Froth 17

Don't Make Her Sad...18

One Day 18

Galaxies For Sale 19

Come Be My Wife..20

Are You My Saviour Or Killer?...21

Let Your Heart Speak 23

Rushing Tears..24

Gods And Poets...26

Don't Ask Me Why I Love You So 28

Love Is Not Blind..29

I Live For You 30

Woman The Puzzle Ultimate 31

Whisper Sweetness In My Ears..33

Women In The Hands Of Men 34

Sigh..35

Beware Of The Small...36

When?..37

Wouldn't Be Fun...38

Only Heroes Die..39

I'm The One For You...40

Young Poets..42

Tiny Shadows 42

Love In Olden Times...43

Addiction Called Love...45

Belief..47

Ladies And Gentlemen..48

I Do...49

Shooting Star..50

God Is Inside...51

Let's Set The Spirits Free..52

Chris And Vicky 52

You Are Amazing!...53

Love Is Cruel...55

Give Birth To Me..56

Sweet And Sour...57

Every Girl Is An Angel..58

I Have Eyes Just For You 59

A Poet's Narrative Of Creation..60

Please Ask Me If I Love You?..62

Poets And Poetry..63

Marriages And Miracles 64

Amorous Advances On Messenger 65

Down With Open Eyes 67

Strange Sensation...67

Why So Far?..68

The Eyes Of Me..69

Kali Kali Zulfon 70

Women And Wine..72

Pain Killer For Love 73

Shining Girls 74

You Ask Me If I Love You...74

You Say You Love Me...75

Who Said I'm Going Away?..76

Forget Tomorrows...77

Good Morning World...78

Life Without A Woman 79

Who Hunts The Hunter?..80

I Saw Your Smile...81
My Lover Is A Wall..82
Next Time We Meet..83
Sex Is A Serious Business..84
High Towers...85
Tit For Tat..86
Foolish Thought Called Love...88
Am I A Bloody Bitch?...90
Waiting Hand...91
Love Is Courage...92
I Am The One For You..93
Burn The Skies With Flames Of Man...................................94
A Place In My Heart...94
One More Day Of Love...95
The Girl From Albania..96
The Spring Of Love..98
A Sea Of Tears..99
The Hardest Prisons Of All..100
Restless Shadows 101
Of All The Girls I Loved..102
Happy Wives..103
Slash 104
With Or Without You..105
Soft Skin..106
A Thousand Years Of Love..107
Muslim Girls..108
Nanny And Grandad...110
Everything I Want To Say..111
Bedtime Story...112
Make Me Happy..114
Just For Me...115
What Gods Created Women?..116
The Shrill Of Love..117
Rameen...118
The Strings Of My Heart...119
The Price Of Truth..120
Bonds Of Love..121
Why Do You Want My Hand?..122

What Can I Do?...123

Vinegar And Wine...124

My Dear..125

The Miracles Of Love..126

Handcuffed By A Ring...127

A Fairy Tale...129

Sit With Me And Cry...130

To Love And Suffer...132

Broken Hearts...133

I Want To Fall In Love..134

Whatever The Bet I'll Play..135

Come Be My Christmas...136

A Novel Read Backwards..137

Life For Most Of Us..139

No Other Reason...140

Where Does Time Go?.. 141

You Know By Now...142

The Waiting Game...142

We Will Be Fine..143

Kings And Queens...143

The Cappuccino Girl...144

Homo Fornicatous...146

Sorrow... 147

You Can't Forget...148

The Price Of Success.. 149

Am I In Love With A Spoon?..151

I Am A Bankrupt Husband,..152

The Greatest Killer...153

Thus Spoke Ziryab (1)..154

Hug Me And Let Me Close My Eyes.................................159

Sometimes...160

Lovers Must Love Every Day... 161

Men Are Doomed To Love Women...................................162

The Joy Of Love... 163

ONLY WHEN DESIRE SCREAMS

All the hours of all the days,
And all the minutes in between,
By all the Gods I'll swear to you
Again and again, I'll love you,
But tread softly,
If you please,
It is not the ground underneath,
It is my heart,
And my soul,
Is just beneath,
So, watch your steps,
The love that can cure us all,
Can also be a disease.

Trust me or fear me not,
If one day,
After a kiss,
Being warm or being hot,
In a moment primed with wonder,
You sigh deep and then you say,
Sweeter than the sweetest wine,
Your lips,
I will remind you, yet again,
Grapes milked for their wine,
Are also milked for vinegar.
Care for me and keep me sweet,
Not every minute of the day,
Not every second of the night,
Not every act; not every deed,
Not every time we will meet,
Only when desire screams,
And all hours of need.

I HEARD IT TOLD

I heard it told,
That a heart in love,
Will never be old.

I heard it sung,
That a woman loved,
And a woman in love,
Is always young.

I heard it said,
That a body may live,
With a broken heart,
But the man inside is dead.

I heard it whispered,
In my ear,
When both so far,
And both so near,
You give me courage to face the world,
But it's you who, I fear.

I read while in bed,
A poet of old who said,
If the hair is grey,
And the money is scarce,
And she is hot,
And you are not,
In her heart,
You are not welcomed,
And so, in a different part.

YOUNG LOVE

Sometimes fast,
And sometimes slow,
Round and round we go,
You may stoop to steal a feel,
I'm ready but don't you dare,
Step on my toe.

Round and round,
And round and round,
Our feet move in haste,
And I wouldn't mind,
If accidently move your hand,
A little below my waist.

If you want to be with me,
I will be with you,
If you want to love me,
I will love you too,
And if you burn with desire,
And your love is really true,
Myself and I will have a talk,
I don't know what is done,
But just in case I knew,
Before each step,
Tell me what you'll do.

SHARE A CHILD

It is not certain what men are born to be,
It all depends on needs,
Sometimes they will be fighters,
In times of peace,
They could be writing poetry.
Girls will be different,
In olden times they will play,
With boys and other girls,
Until they reach puberty,
The playing field is abandoned,
To join the kingdom of women,
The sole creators of humanity.

It does look to all who think,
Given time boys will be men,
And look it does,
Even before they are girls,
They know they are mums.
Not all men are lucky,
Not all girls are blessed,
Men need women to love,
And women will need maternity,
So go on if you can,
And go on if you can't,
Create a child or share a child,
Women are the only means,
To give us eternity.

PREGNANT

Come take my hand and dance,
But hold me close,
I feel light, as if in a trance,
Or better still,
Come next to me,
Press your lips against my lips,
Let's melt them in a kiss,
And let's see where it takes us,
Here is good and so is bed,
Or else,
Push your shoulder a bit,
And let me rest my head,
A new life I'm creating,
Is glowing with a silvery light,
Everything that comes to mind,
And everything I see,
Appear to bring me peace,
And make me feel glad,
Now I know how it feels,
To create life,
And be a glorious god.

FOR YOU AND FOR ME

Read me and judge me,
Don't judge me and read,
I need to fall in love with you,
But it's not my only need,
I'm doing all I can,
And some I should not,
I cheated so you'd love me more,
For God's sake so what?
I am a woman in love,
More clean in body,
And more pure in heart,
Than all the saints you know on Earth,
And all the gods above.

I AM WOMAN,

I am the truth,
And truth for me is love,
A lover now and mum I'll be,
And now, tomorrow and every day,
For that I'll do it all,
For me and for you,
Or else, if you choose,
Just for me.

NEW EQUILIBRIUM

You may say we are now in a new equilibrium;
All the characters are in predetermined places;
Nothing has remained,
But for the curtains to be raised;
The dancing floor is ready;
The projectors are in action;
The orchestra started playing; its members are looking at the audience, urging all to stop wasting time and walk to the dancing floor.

Everything is ready for the young man to take a deep breath, stand tall, lift his head up and walk in firm steps into the dancing floor, then extend his hand, pull the girl out of her hesitation, take her palm into his right, wrap his left arm around her waist and whisper in her ear.

Once the introduction is over,
they will dance for a long time.
He'll try to take her into a corner,
Where nobody can hear a whisper.
And there ...
there he will press his lips against her ear and pour out his heart.
She won't say a word;
And their eyes will not meet,
But her shoulders will grow wings of happiness,
And take her off her feet.

All the girls he loved before,
Now they know it's over,
And one or two may say: He loved me before, but in his heart no more.

FAMILY

If one day you feel lonely,
And you ask yourself why,
Leave your room and out you go,
And peer at the sky.
That's where you came from,
And that's where you'll go,
One particle at a time,
Of fine cosmic dust,
Of origin sacred,
And creation divine,
You may feel lonely,
And that's all right,
But you are not alone,
No one is,
Everywhere you look,
Everything you see,
Is family.

JUST SAY "SORRY"

If ever you are in doubt,
What love is all about,
Don't break your heart,
And go for the primeval,
Make a telephone call,
You know he is waiting,
Your gesture will be nice,
And before you say "I'm sorry",
He'll probably say it twice,
You'll chat again in silence,
Or out you may go,
Encourage him with a kiss,
Hold his hand and shake it,
Laugh and confess,
That you did it twice, or more,
But this time you wouldn't fake it,
Come with me,
You'll say,
It will only cost you a latte,
But the bed is free,
And so is me,
And whatever you ask,
Will be.

I SEE DESIRE IN YOUR EYES

I see desire in your eyes,
So don't deny, complain or fret,
I understand what is meant,
The hearts won't bond,
Unless the bodies do,
I may not show it,
But strong my desire too,
But it won't happen,
So please relax,
Or curse away if you must,
My ears are tightly shut,
Until you know my sesame word,
Failing that prove to me,
You have a heart I trust.
My sesame key is a four-letter word,
And yours, thus far, is three,
When you remove the 'c',
What's good for you,
For me may not be,
So, choose your word carefully,
I'll listen,
You can persist,
But I'll say it again,
When you're welcomed in my heart,
You'll be welcomed in my body,
I am ME,
I will make the final call,
And what will be will be.

LIFE IS GREAT

Sadness is not ordained,
And grief is not our fate,
One day soon to your heart,
Joy will find its way,
You'll be happy you are alive,
And life will be great.

In each of us there's a call,
Marked "invitation to all",
It's not a postcard or a letter,
There isn't a box for it,
It's an issue by the heart,
Usually conveyed by the eyes,
And understood by those who see.

You can't open a heart,
From behind closed doors,
You can't wait for it,
You have to go out,
Present yourself with an open hand,
And a heart more open,
"Here it is, take it."
I am the one for you,
And you are the one for me,
Come join in a journey,
Life is great,
Let's play our part,
Be with me,
When you do,
Both we will BE.

GO TO HELL

Time is a young man's friend,
And an old man's enemy,
It is a case of what has been,
And a case of what will be,
It is a river's vibrant flow,
And an aging waveless sea,
But that's not all,
A great deal has been seen,
And very few to tell,
No regrets are there,
No pain,
And no hell,
Once is enough,
There's no will,
To see them again,
In summing up I would say,
If you offer youth again,
I'll tell you to go away,
If you persist,
I'll tell you to go to hell,
One life is long enough,
Another I will kill.

HAND IN HAND

I've never seen,
A dreamy scene,
So clear,
Footsteps so light,
Inside my heart,
I hear,
And whispers sweet,
Enticing souls to twine,
And dreams to blend,
And lips so finely dewed by waiting,
And parched by desire,
For far, far too long,
Finally,
Oh, finally my life and my joy,
Finally, will meet.
Then silence reigns until the chest heaves out,
Will you be mine one day,
Will I be yours?
Will we be free of gnawing fear,
And doubt,
Doomed to feel,
Sometimes too far we are,
Sometimes too near?
There's a road ahead,
A road that will be,
Let's take a walk along the course of fate,
So that She may see,
That hand in hand I am with you,
And you at last with me,
A bonding love,
Shall always set,
Two loving hearts free.

BREATHLESS

Breathless I shall wait,
In the shadows; in the light,
And as I see her standing there,
The brightest moon in a darkened night,
I feel suspended with my stare.
Like the bud of an anxious rose,
The love I feel for her unfolds,
With scented passions set alight,
Blink not, eyes, for there she goes,
And soon you'll have her in your sight.
My heart is open, open wide,
And she's already deep inside,
Soft as a whisper and softer still,
Her gentle touch and magic thrill,
Fills my heart with joy,
Like that I used to feel,
As Christmas finally comes,
When I was a boy.

My soul and hers eternally meet,
In a long, breathless, wandering kiss,
A state of bliss:
Two hearts are bound in a single beat,
Two separate souls are jointly crowned,
And breathing rhymes with a single sound,
A state of love:
A pure state of love –
What else?

WHO WANTS TO BE A GOD?

What does it mean,
To never bond with men,
And never melt with women,
To know no pals,
No lovers, no family,
No kith and no kin?

What does it mean,
To have no friend,
No dad and no mum,
No start and no end?

This's the price you have to pay,
If you want to be a god,
Hail to them for the sacrifice,
Let's be kind and cheer them up,
All of them are envious,
All of them are lonely,
And all of them are sad.

FROTH

If you are to choose,
Go for the easiest,
Life is too short,
So do what's possible,
Then have a rest.
Towards the end of life,
You begin to realise,
Your greatest achievements,
Are the children you have,
And only through their eyes,
And those of their children,
You'll see what they see,
And you will remain alive,
All that remains is froth,
One day you'll be buried,
In a soiled, dirty cloth,
Always is wet,
While your bones are dry,
Under a spot in a cemetery,
Where dogs love to shit.

DON'T MAKE HER SAD

You think it's a lot,
But there will be a time,
When you know it is not,
Where did the years go?
You'll ask yourself,
Again, again and again,
As if you are stupid,
Or don't really know,
Or somehow forgotten their pain.
Do yourself a favour,
Make her happy,
And she will make you glad,
If you can't for any reason,
Tell her: love, please be patient;
I grieve when you are said.

ONE DAY

One day the sea's heart may stop beating,
For reasons awesome, the world may go cold,
Springs and summers may not be meeting,
And Earth may dwarf and grow finally old.
The wind, tired of blowing, may at last cease,
Birds lose their wings, butterflies and bees,
The greenery of leaves may fade and rust,
And all living things may turn to dust.
But my love, dear LOVE, will forever grow,
Past all the limits Man and Time may know,
Past the failing heart of sea and wind,
Past creatures' life when they come to an end,
A promise of eternal love I here pledge thee,
Ours is not just today but every day is anniversary.

GALAXIES FOR SALE

Can someone with a better mind,
Please explain,
What's the point of galaxies,
Where boys and girls have no fun,
Birds are never seen,
Skies pour no rain,
And children can't run?

And why so many?
Billions, billions and billions,
Of useless objects in flight,
Not a single song was ever heard,
And not a single soul in sight?

There's mayhem out there,
A senseless war between the stars,
The end of which no one can tell,
Let's lie and call it Heaven,
Or let's be honest and call it "hell",
No friends are there for us,
Bastards all of them,
The largest and the small,
And all are biding time,
One day dark and ugly,
A jealous asteroid of Earth,
Will kill us all.

Call me a fool or call me funny,
For a child's smile,
I'll empty all my pockets,
For all the galaxies of the world,
I'll pay not a penny.

COME BE MY WIFE

Let me share your joy and sorrow,
And you can share my dreams,
A bit today and a bit tomorrow,
Like the raindrops of streams,
And with all the dreams,
Let there be wine,
And with wine a sweet pledge,
I'll be yours forever,
If forever you'll be mine,
Like night and day,
Like Earth and Moon,
Forever intertwined,
Like skies and stars,
Like sea and land,
Always hand in hand.
Like a sailor and his boat,
A thinker and his mind,
And all others combined.

Come dance with me,
Come laugh with me,
Come live with me,
Come cry with me,
Come share my life,
Come be my wife,
Come be a joy gone wild,
Come be the most beautiful mum,
For a most beautiful child.

ARE YOU MY SAVIOUR OR KILLER?

Like night sleepy at sunrise,
I'm always dreaming in your arms,
Stretch both and take me in,
Drift in my heart like a dream,
Step by step like the morning mist,
Drop by drop like a stream,
Bring me along the sweet surprise,
The wistful looks of dreamy eyes,
The pouting lips in a daring smile,
Surreal, my girl you are,
Surreal and yet so real,
And the princess of your kind.

With face angelic and eyes stellar,
Are you my saviour or killer,
I'll be happy with either choice,
The moment you make up your mind,
Until you do, come take my hand,
I feel I need to dance,
I'll sweep you off your feet,
And you can sweep off my mind,
With a kiss send me in a trance,
Wingless like a dream I seem,
Always, always ready to fly.

Press your lips against my lips,
Then let my heart flow,
With the sweetest words ever told;
Stand on a cushion of air,
And really, really slow,
Around the sweetest of all dreams,
Round and round we go,

My heart is screaming,
But in whispers I will say:
Take me now,
I'll be with you,
Forever true,
Till the end of time,

Be with me,
Come be with me,
You'll see,
The best is yet to be,
I promise,
And if you want me to,
I'll cross my heart,
For that I need it,
I know you'll say, «no way Jose»,
But I can't do without,
And just for only ten seconds,
Let me have it back.

LET YOUR HEART SPEAK

Don't ever say, "I love you,"
Unless you really do,
The downsize is impossible,
The upgrade "I do,"
It's a primeval legacy,
From very ancient lovers,
The meaning we take lightly,
Is "my heart I give to you."

For every girl a chance to take,
For every boy a bet,
Don't rush but wisely chose,
The choice sometimes you think is best,
Is the one you should reject.

Whose fault it was it matters not,
The fault already is made,
Forgive yourself but you should know,
Mistakes of love have a price,
Never is fully paid.

This old lover will tell you,
When time to fall in love arrives,
Choose the words unique,
Open your eyes,
Shut your mouth,
And let your heart speak.

RUSHING TEARS

A glass of milk for breakfast,
A chocolate bar for lunch,
Supper with a glass of wine,
I've never asked for much,
A walk would do me fine,
All the streets are mine,
There you see some faces,
Ready to cry for a touch,
And velvet, secretive places,
Some eyes invite me to watch,
And I always find out there,
What makes me stop and watch,
I want to help all people,
To rejoice with loud cheers,
But one can do so much,
To stop their streaming tears.

The sky is turning dark,
The light is fading fast,
Across the deserted park,
It looks as if midnight,
A garden's bench is now,
A young woman's retreat,
Holding a folded paper,
Creased by a tight squeeze,
And only when light flashes,
I see her rushing tears.

A man alone at a table,
Sad with an empty stare,
Here and yet somewhere,
Gazing at an empty chair,
Is this the final end?

All along she knew?
What would it take to be friends?
What would it take to be true?
What words are there to say?
What else is there to do?

He will remain in love,
Waiting for an hour or two,
Then slowly shuts his heart,
Nothing is left to do,
Life the bitch is never fair,
And love is never true,
Hurt and cheat each other,
And that's what we do,

All lovers beware,
Once in your heart,
Always will be there,
It's not ink you can wipe,
Its name is burnt on the wall,
It hurts every time you look,
And wants nothing or all.
You think you can forget,
You are wrong,
You can try,
And you can lie,
Nobody does,
And you can't too.

GODS AND POETS

And Princess Nailamar said, "Men are like the grains of sand we have now as our rug. From afar they all look alike until you come closer and inspect them in the sun, and only then you will see men and you will see men with hearts."

And Princess Nailamar said, "If Allah dislikes a man, he gives him wealth so all men with poor hearts may hate him. And if Allah loves a man, he gives him the gift of poetry so all men with rich hearts may love him. That is their reward for him in life and thereafter, but God rewards him even more. His spirit will be permitted to wander in His gardens as he pleases, and when he's ready with his next poem He will get all his angels and listen in silence again and marvel at the mighty power he has created out of simple words for God too is good at creating marvels out of simple things.

"And the boy said, "But if the Almighty Allah wants a man to be loved and hated at the same time, what would He do?"

And Princess Nailamar said, "He gives him a woman. He gives him a woman and says: Know! You will be the pillar of the house but your woman will be the foundations. And He tells him: Know that quakes always rumble from beneath. And know that her hatred can be great so do not make her beg for money or for tenderness for I made these and others the secret way to her heart, and to the best of the means I have given you, make both flow like a spring not squeezed out of you like a lemon for then I will make you squeeze out sustenance from me and comfort from your woman and you will be always hungry for both and bitter."

And the boy asked, "And what does He say to the woman?"

"To the woman," Princess Nailamar said, "he has a more important message. And he says to her: Know! People expect of me to be with them and look after them every minute of the day and night and bring them food and comfort, and I do. They always look up to find me but little they know I am everywhere but most of all in them and amongst them. And through agents of mine on Earth they call women I provide all this and more. And He tells her: Know! I have given you all my love and all my anger, and I entrusted you with men and children not because you are the strongest but because they are the weakest. For that I love them no less and, like a father, my attention will always be given to the weak until they are stronger, and to the sick until they recover so restrain your anger and make your love unrestrained. And if your bosom should heave with your hatred for him, and it will, remember that quakes do bring down the walls and rooftops of homes but they all come crashing down on the very foundations that shook them into sand. And if you do all that I expect of you, you too will be permitted to wander in my gardens as you please, and you will be loved by me and all my angels for I am the creator of all living things but women, my agent, are the maker of poets and good men."

DON'T ASK ME WHY I LOVE YOU SO

Don't ask me why I love you so,
But tell me why I should,
If I know I'll let you know,
But only if I could.

What I know I loved you more,
Than all of them before,
Maybe something in your eyes,
The way you talked,
The way you joked,
The way you danced,
The way you kissed,
And maybe even more,
You made me feel I was safe,
And no matter what,
Until the last of days,
I will be loved.

I used to think that all in all,
We had a lucky start,
But now I feel and sometimes fear,
It was the easy part.
So, work it in or work it out,
In the shadows, in the light,
Plan it if you need to plan,
Make your way, or cheat your way,
Win me every way you can,
I don't care,
And I don't mind,
Love was and always will be,
Our greatest dare,
I am with you all the way,

In every way,
And every minute of every day,
Because I locked you in my heart,
And need you there,
To stay.

LOVE IS NOT BLIND

Love is not blind,
Intuitive it can be,
It senses and it feels,
But no eyes that can see,
And neither logic nor reason,
Are taken seriously.
Love has two eyes,
One gives and one takes,
To count the merits is open,
And closed will be the one,
That looks for mistakes.
Love's power to change is huge,
But it needs time,
And courage even more,
Judge love after love,
You can't judge it before,
To see inside is to be inside,
For that you need a door,
Most will cross it and fall in love,
Some hesitate and love will be not,
The closed eye will open,
But the door will be shut.

I LIVE FOR YOU

Ask me something,
I should do,
Or you should do,
Whatever it is,
Just do it,
Of course, I will,
Whatever you'll do,
Whatever you'll say,
Now, tomorrow,
And forever,
I will obey,
But only because,
I live for you,
And deep inside I really know,
You live for me,
And you do know,
I live for you,
And I hesitate not a bit,
So, what the heck!
Let's do it,
Life is short for all lovers,
It could be many scores of years,
But one day it will end,
Just before you know it,
It's one way,
Called love,
What other roads are there for us?
What else,
Is there to say,
Except: I love you,
And I will always,
Live for you?

WOMAN THE PUZZLE ULTIMATE

Of all men,
Nobody more than poets,
Ever loved women.
Their skin is not actually silk,
Nor their lips are petals,
Or their eyes shooting stars,
And their kiss,
Sweeter than the sweetest wine,
No less,
But they are women,
Not exactly edible,
But close enough,
And some have curves,
That can drive a saint saint-less,
And sane men numb and senseless,
With just a twist or a sway,
In a very pleasant way.
Women invented gods,
To help conquer men,
And like cattle,
With stifled moans,
Men are driven to temples,
To pray for a doll,
Or a pile of chiselled stones,
Halleluiah, they repeat, Halleluiah,
For what?
They have no idea.
Or else!
No food for you; no sex,
Their wives will tell them,
And sheepishly say, "yes."

So, are they liars,
All poets, I mean?
Far from it, it's all true.
Poets don't see women,
What they see are dreams,
Enshrined in a promise,
And a most mysterious puzzle.
People read the words,
But poets write the dreams.
It's not sex, it's not the food,
It's not the laughs,
It's not the mood,
What women give men,
Is something magical,
Neither is aware,
Of its essence,
Or why?
It's eternity,
Folks,
Eternity, no less.
That's why Arabians say,
Those who have children,
Will always have the bless,
Because they'll never die.
Through the eyes,
Of their kids,
The future will be seen,
And its days shall be lived,
Again, again and again,
Every time a child is born,
A new life to them is given.
Poets know this,
And that's why,
They'll always love women,

More than anybody else.
Women are a puzzle, all right,
Like their plumbing system,
But isn't that what creation,
Of all puzzles the ultimate?
God created the universe,
And women created us,
And that's why,
We'll never die,
And if men are kind to them,
And love them above all else,
They will happily continue,
To do just this.

WHISPER SWEETNESS IN MY EARS

Men sometimes amaze me,
And drive me round the bend,
For the rubbish they repeat,
That a woman is a mystery book,
Impossible to comprehend.

I'm a woman and I understand,
If I do anybody can,
If you love me,
Wait for an hour of need,
Then hold me tight,
Whisper sweetness in my ears,
Then close your eyes,
And read.

WOMEN IN THE HANDS OF MEN

Like orange peel,
Men for girls,
Can pollute and clean,
In their hands,
A girl becomes a woman,
And soon enough a pauper,
Or before long a queen.
So, treat gently,
With respect,
Petals of a rose,
Are easily detached,
But not re-attached,
The sadness never ends,
With no queen in the beehive,
The heart may shrivel and dim,
The winter is long,
But it will survive,
Then comes along,
Another man,
With gentleness and love,
Slowly, the heart will wake up,
And begins to revive,
At last, at last,
A new queen is alive,
And soon enough,
Both will begin to thrive,
And a family becomes the beehive.

SIGH

Tell me that I make mistakes,
Don't tell me that I lie,
My love for you needs no proof,
And you know exactly why,
There's nothing for me to hide,
The only thing I really want,
The only dream I'll ever have,
Is to be at your side.

Sometimes I'm filled with fears,
When you begin to cry,
Your smile is forced,
But not at all your sigh,
Will you be mine for ever?
Will I be yours?
Or will we for some foolish thoughts,
And many imagined doubts,
Turn off the flames of love,
And let it slowly die?

Tell me what I always tell you:
As long as we're together,
We will be fine,
I will be yours forever,
And you will be mine.

BEWARE OF THE SMALL

Don't be sad,
Everything we do,
Is either good or bad,
And neither lasts,
You will have a day,
When for a mistake,
A price you will pay,
In another for a good deed,
A reward you will take,
Even the longest night will end,
And of all the ugly times,
One at least will be friend,
Constant is a myth,
Nothing is,
Even eternity will end,
And you will need to change,
Don't fight the sea,
Ride its waves to your shore,
If not, changed you will be,
The one before is no more,
The one after is unknown,
At worst a faceless shadow,
At best a mere clone,
And for a while,
It is good to be alone,
They know your weakest point,
And the blow of your dearest,
Is the hardest of all,
And they will be the first,
To ignore an anguished call,
And the last to wish you well,

As they wait for you to fall,
They'll never change,
Look up if you want to look,
And beware of the small.

WHEN?

When the night is full of fear,
And the day full of fright,
Take me in your arms and tell me:
Don't worry my dearest darling,
These are difficult times for us,
But we will be all right,

When the worries are far too many,
And weakened is the heart,
Take me in your arms and tell me:
Don't worry my dearest darling.
My heart will beat for you and I,
And you will be all right.

WOULDN'T BE FUN

Wouldn't be fun,
If,
After a shower,
Every memory you don't want,
Is washed away and gone?

Wouldn't be great,
If the love of your life,
Called to say,
When you were away,
She has to wed a friend,
Because her period is far too late,
Will call again,
To say she changed her mind,
And she will wait?

What road should one take,
Except memory lane?
Call it what you will,
For far too many,
It is a slow road to hell,
Lined by windows closed,
And hearts full of pain,
Fed by tears that flow,
Until the eyes bulge,
But only for a while,
From where?
No one knows,
Will rush again.

Was I who betrayed or was it you?
From both silence long,
Shattered by a cry,
Neither knew who's to blame,
But both screamed "why"?
There's something wrong with all of this,
The gods were bored,
Pots primed with holy liquid,
Were kicked around and emptied,
And out came the world.
It may take a while,
But shrivel one day it will,
And soon it will die,
And blink, blink,
All of us in hell.

ONLY HEROES DIE

Alone is not lonely,
Alone are the brave,
Lonely is a dying soul,
Without the comfort of a grave,
The cowards will always make it,
And they will live another day,
On the battlefields of life,
Only heroes die,
And as all others celebrate victory,
Their mums begin to cry.

I'M THE ONE FOR YOU

Is this really what love being?
I call to say good night,
And he said it's far too late?
We can't rush love,
He says,
So, I'll have to wait.
Fine!
If not pigs,
Some men are swine,
I can wait,
But my youth can't,
Nor indeed my charm,
For him or anybody else,
I'm not willing to trade both,
For a pile of wasted time,
If he needs me to explain,
With stats and charts,
For God's sake do!
But do it alone,
I'm sorry,
I wasted your time,
And you've wasted mine,
So, run along and grow up,
I talked to a boy,
A boy is not a man,
A man will understand,
If he doesn't have a wife,
He'll be living,
But he won't have a life,
He'll also understand,
A good woman is not a bus,
If missed,

In ten minutes,
Another will be found,
Blink and look
All vanished,
For all of you, little men,
No one is around,
For all others,
Those who'll say to us,
We're men,
And understand we do,
I'm willing to raise my hand,
For all to see,
Wave to you,
And shout,
Wait no more,
Loved one,
I'm the one for you,
And whatever faults you have,
Perfectly you will do.

YOUNG POETS

Summer's warmth is long forgotten,
In the midst of winter's cold,
And fleeing youth is a distant shadow,
And so soon we'll grow old.
The band must keep playing,
To have her maiden dance,
Waltzing eyes in gentle crying,
May give poets another chance.
If their words are truly bold,
They will be eternally sung,
And if their hearts are truly young,
They'll never grow old.

TINY SHADOWS

Old is not dying,
Old is to prepare yourself,
For the day when you will,
Have courage, stand tall,
And look death in the eye,
Scream at him you are ready,
I said to the hated live in peace,
And said to the loved goodbye,
I am finished with my body,
Take it now or by all the gods,
I'll grab what's left of it,
And throw it at your face,
A tiny spark will disengage,
Waves to me and fly away.

LOVE IN OLDEN TIMES

Love is not to blame,
For being born with a brighter flame,
In older times it was the norm,
In ours it's not the same.
In eons past life was hard,
Half the babies didn't survive,
And short were parents' lives,
First one and then the other,
And the older would be twenty-five,
The flames of love are far too bright,
To only live on memory,
Of times that once were,
And like the body of a silent candle,
Neither light nor warmth are there,
Some will live and play their part,
Those who can't will shut down,
And die of a broken heart.

With three times the average age,
Of times gone,
Is there life in old love,
For joy or for fun?
What is it if not?
A painting of young lovers,
Who never age?
Is it a book,
Without an end,
One day will be reached,
Page after page?

The ancients did not say,
For them life, love and heart,
Derive from a single root,
Living and loving were the same,
There was no other way.
There is life in old love,
Though subdued and tamed,
No sparks are there,
To burn the skies,
No cracks on the wall,
And the ceiling is confident,
Whatever they do won't cause a fall,
With dentures firmly in place,
Bites don't hurt,
And the bitten is not the bait,
Blunt is the flirt,
Strange sounds are often heard,
And the moves are confused,
One asks the other to turn over,
While he's turning round,
The come is far too early,
And the go is far too late,
The mattress doesn't ache,
And the bed is oblivious,
Mournful of times,
When henges were dislodged,
And implored by wild screams,
To speed it up and break.

ADDICTION CALLED LOVE

Standing on your head,
You may begin to see things,
As clearly as you should,
What you thought is rare,
Is actually far too common,
And what's common is rare,
Nightmares are dreams unpleasant,
And pleasant dreams are wishful thinking,
Full of lies and air,
And twisted shadows of happiness,
created by despair.
The sky is a desert,
No water there,
And nothing is cruel or fair,
And as lonely as a star,
You long,
Her arm is seen stretched,
All the way to you,
And all the way stretched,
Is your arm,
But can't touch,
No matter what you do,
They will remain too far,
The love that cures,
Will begin to harm.

This's what girls are good at,
Taught by their mums,
And in every case is seen,
Suckle, suckle, suckle, suckle,
Until the addiction is complete,
And then begins the wean.

It's not the mild bite of a snake,
Nor the strong sting of a bee,
It's a natural process of deprivation,
You have to wait and see,
Devised to destabilise,
For what reason it's hard to say,
It could be a simple statement,
It's time you know who you are,
And time to know who's me.
As long as they're happy,
You have your head high,
And feet low,
The moment they are not,
They switch,
You walk on your head,
And you think with your feet,
Nothing is nothing of what it was,
And everything is tasteless,
Nothing is of value,
And even life itself can be,
Either worth nothing,
Or much less.

Things you miss are not the same,
As those you may wish,
And craving is even more,
They were facts but ceased,
And list what you miss,
You will be overwhelmed,
It's not just sex,
Nor the cuddle and the kiss,
Not the smiles or the frowns,
Or the gentle sound of steps,
It is not the company or the bother,

It's everything you miss,
And much more than that,
It's not just the missing,
It is a crave.
It could be more,
And it could be less,
Addictions can be deadly,
And those of love are serious,
Too late for stops and starts,
Or too early to their grave,
Some with broken bodies and souls,
And some with broken hearts.

BELIEF

My mind is anxious to believe,
But my heart worships you,
Tell me after a longer kiss,
Which ones are false gods?
And which one is true?

LADIES AND GENTLEMEN

Gentlemen are made by ladies,
And good homes by dedicated mums,
If mums want dedicated husbands,
They should be dedicated wives,
For only both can make a garden,
And that's where a lady thrives.

Some men enjoy some culture,
Others would want a simple life,
And there're those seeking adventure,
And still more a loving wife,
But you may choose to have all that,
If you choose a very good wife.
Not before long we'll be old,
Body and youth will grow apart,
But for youth this isn't an end,
And it could be another start,
For it will live in a withering garden,
But it will die in a withering heart.

I DO

If bonds of love,
are made above,
is true,
then why resist,
I have the best,
the only man,
I want to love,
Is you.

I should with care,
deal with an affair,
so new,
but what the heck,
you make me tick,
the only man,
who makes me dare,
Is you.
At times, before,
I had a doubt,
or two,
but when once more,
after your kiss,
instead of no,
I whispered yes,
I knew.

I knew that love will come one day,
And take my doubts and fears away,
I never thought it will be so soon,
There was no music, dance or moon,
And not even words to say.

And when you took me in your arms,
And love twinkled in your eyes,
I knew you love me like I do,
How did you make me fall for you?
I never planned for it this way.

But if bonds of love,
Are made above,
Is true,
Why wait?
I took the bait,
I want to take,
Your hand one day,
And gaze at you,
and thrillingly say,
I do.

SHOOTING STAR

Every star,
Large or small,
Has a living human soul,
If you see a shooting star,
Hold your breath,
For they may call:
Have courage,
Our little ones,
God bless,
We miss you all.

GOD IS INSIDE

Behind the stern façade,
Sits silent a scared child,
What is he afraid of?
Doesn't he know,
No worse than a monkey,
Amongst all our relatives,
Was re-created by a god?
If monkey, so what?
Monkey was and monkey is,
And they say in Arabic *tozz*.
If the boy looks around,
He may eventually find,
That God is inside,
Earth is heavenly,
And heaven is hell,
Where else would he be?
Like the soft warmth,
Of the touch of a loving hand,
His would be the same,
To feel it, be as loving,
He can forgive,
Because you and him are one,
So, forgive yourself,
We all make mistakes,
He did once,
If you want to know which one,
Fetch a mirror and look at us,
If you forgive yourself,
You are forgiven,
To pay for it,
Forgive God again,
And forgive somebody,
God will be thrilled,
And all will be happy.

LET'S SET THE SPIRITS FREE

Our bodies are tied,
By the shackles of time,
Let's set the spirits free,
Let's demolish a faulty setup,
Of five thousand years,
With the aim to control,
With threats and with fears,
What's left of our body,
And they leave of our soul,
Kings rule on Earth,
Priests rule in heaven,
It's time for us to realise,
That priests and kings are liars,
And hell, and heaven are lies.

CHRIS AND VICKY

Two miracles in the sky were seen,
And people rushed to greet,
One of them was glorious green,
The other white and pink,
And wings were her feet,
The first filled the hearts with bless,
And people said: «from this moment,
He'll be called Chris,»
The other was truly pretty,
And henceforth, they all agreed,
She'll be known as Vicky.

YOU ARE AMAZING!

Reluctantly,
She closed her book,
and as hard as she could,
she heard his steps,
and fought the urge to look.
She stacked her books neatly,
and held in both hands,
she raised her head,
on the elegant body of a swan,
and stood:
What now desires my shadow?
Every day of last week,
You asked to borrow my books,
The semantics of words I know you know,
And the syntax that I don't,
This morning you surprised me;
With a thrilled voice and high,
You said I look amazing,
Surprised,
No one in the class laughed,
Except you and I,
And now you come for something,
I have nothing for borrowing,
And nothing you really need,

I do, my most amazing girl, he said,
I really, really do,
In whole and in part indeed,
You are everything I need,
And now I'll ask for all of them:
Can I have your heart?
I can't, she said, blushing,

Hearts are not given,
If you really want my heart,
You may try to take it,
But I like you,
So I'll cheat and tell you how:

Be kind to me and good,
And true, please be,
You may look at all the girls,
But only think of me,
And I myself will do,
Be careful what you tell me,
My soul is soft,
And I need to be prepared,
Private sins will bury themselves,
Unless they are shared,
Share with me what makes you happy.
And I will share my joy,
My heart I can't give,
Unless sure of you.

That was before but after,
I don't know what I was thinking,
I must have swallowed and blinked,
When I shouldn't,
And before I knew,
I reached for my heart with fear,
But happily, I found out,
Half of it was willingly stolen,
By a most amazing boy,
I'll keep the other half for now,
And when he'll reach for it one day,
I'll pretend I didn't see,
And quickly look away.

LOVE IS CRUEL

Love is cruel,
Now I have no doubt,
But for what reason,
You add your cruelty to that?
Is mending ways difficult,
But easy to break a heart?

The stream of love,
Once I thought,
Forever will flow,
Is desert dry,
Even the mirage is no more,
And burning is the sky,
Is there an end to tears?
Or doomed I am,
To an endless cry?

I thought I knew what love is,
Now I know I don't.
Sometimes it's a key to free,
And times a key to chain,
Sometimes joy and happiness,
And sometimes full of pain,
It's pot luck, love is,
Damn it!
And I should love less and less,
So, I don't know,
Whatever for,
I seem to love you more?

GIVE BIRTH TO ME

You are the perfect woman,
I confess,
And you have the right to demand,
Absolutely nothing else,
But nonetheless,
Both of us are creations,
Inside the same womb,
But sometimes I wonder,
Are we?
I am born to be the hunter,
And you the hunted one,
Mother nature is wrong,
Let's change the rules,
You'll be the willing hunter
And I the willing prey.
I'm not the perfect man,
I confess,
But for God's sake,
My perfect girl,
You are a mum,
Give birth to me,
And make me one,
Then, like you,
I'll drop my head in respect,
For my perfect girl,
And say:
Let's do it,
The future is bright,
For all perfect men,
And all women,
Perfect when are born,
Life is great,

And happiness with no end,
Will be the gift for both of us,
And all of us,
Amen.

SWEET AND SOUR

No stronger tie than love is known,
No sweeter taste and sour,
Nothing like two loving lips,
Can have disarming power,
You said it first so I'll repeat,
Lovers young and lovers old,
Stand tall when you meet,
The sky is just below your heads,
And the world at your feet.

EVERY GIRL IS AN ANGEL

If your love should come one day,
And thunders he will go away,
Don't cry.
The worst mistake,
A stupid man,
Can ever make,
Is to leave his girl in tears,
And here's why:
 Every girl's an angel,
 Every girl's a dream,
 Every girl's a raindrop,
 Waiting for a stream.
 Every girl's a fairy-tale,
 One day will to be told,
 If your love should me cry,
 Take me; tightly hold.
 Love is like a candle light,
 Burn it really slow,
 If the world should make me dim,
 Love me; make me glow.
I will love,
I will love,
I will love and love again,
Like no one loved before,
And if more love will give me pain,
I will love you more.
I Will Love
I Will Love
I will love and love again,
Forever and ever more,
And when at last we're together,
Tell me you will too.

Take my hand and lead me on,
Gently like a stream,
Close my eyes with a magic kiss,
And wake me for my dream,
Wake Me for My Dream.

(A song)

I HAVE EYES JUST FOR YOU

I look around and see you not,
And no one there that I can see,
Tell me again what did you do,
It's as if that since we met,
My eyes are there just for you.

I look at you and see just you,
And no one else that I can see,
Tell me again what did you do,
It's as if that since we met,
Cross-eyed I am just of you.

A POET'S NARRATIVE OF CREATION

(1)
God created heavens and earth,
But his work was not done,
Nor did he rest on the sixth day,
Until he created woman.

(2)
On the 7th day,
God called his daughter,
"My work was finished,
When your work began,
And from the womb I gave you,
You will create your man,
And the moment you are two,
Forever and ever,
You'll belong to him,
And forever and ever,
He'll belong to you."

(3)
Dearest father, said the daughter,
What you asked is done,
But both of us are weak,
And we will be alone,
And I'm afraid,
To wake up one day,
And find he is gone,
The only one,
I want to need,
The only one I want to love,

Is you,
Whose help shall I seek,
If that becomes true,
And you were away,
What then will I do?

(4)
The Father thought like a father,
And spoke like a father too:
"You are my only daughter,
And the only one I made,
You created Adam,
So, he belongs to you,
And heart and soul,
And soul and mind,
Sometimes you'll be two,
And sometimes you'll be one,
A new life will be created,
By the two of you,
And just like mine,
Your work will be done."

PLEASE ASK ME IF I LOVE YOU?

Ask me, my love,
If I love you?
The love I have in my heart,
Does not know yet,
How to speak out,
But oh! My love,
If only you know,
How much love,
I have for you,
Then you may have some pity,
And tell me what to do.

God! You've forgiven us all our sins,
And for each you've shown us mercy,
My sin is that I love him,
Tell my longing for my sin,
To have some mercy on me.

2

It is unfair that I should burn,
By the love I have for him,
My God who's in Heaven,
You are Just and you are Fair,
And you are Right, and you are True,
Order my love to love me,
So, with the fire of my love,
I can burn him too.

Translation of the first and last lines of the first stanza of a poem in Arabic by Adel.

POETS AND POETRY

Don't dig the grave,
And prepare to bury,
The heart of gender literary,
We can't expect a towering tree,
If cracked is the seed,
The age of Twitter and Facebook,
Produced in bulk and speed,
Far too many poets,
And far too little poetry.

Not every word that comes to mind,
Is worth writing down,
Not every tear is genuine,
Not every sky is blue,
Not everything that people say,
Can make sense,
Not every love is true,
A great deal of what we hear,
And we read is fake,
And yes, go ahead and read the books,
But perhaps you should know,
That all the books ever written,
Will not a poet make.

Listen to the body and hear its words,
And always watch the eye,
The mouth is a notorious liar,
But the eye will never lie,
The essence of what we want to say,
Is not carried by words,
But the unique feelings they convey,
When complete your homework,

And you have done your part,
Sit down and re-think them all,
Sharpen pencils and fill your pen,
Then write with your heart.

MARRIAGES AND MIRACLES

Some marriages are made in Heaven,
And some are made in hell,
Every day is dark or darker,
And every night is darker still,
There are times to be sober,
And there are times to be drunk,
Sober is a marriage of bliss,
Drunk is a marriage of junk,
Happiness real is happiness made,
It's not a feeling we can fake,
Love to us is a gifted miracle,
Marriage is a miracle you must make.

AMOROUS ADVANCES ON MESSENGER

So, on Messenger,
James Mary was back again,
"Sir," she said, "how old are you?"
I said, "Even if I grossly lie,
and by all means I will,
reduce it by three,
then divide it by two,
I'll still be older than Noah,
And far too old for you."

She laughed and then she said,
"Don't worry, sir.
I can handle young and old,
and, sir, I can tell you this:
I find the young bloody cowards,
and the old bloody bold,
and no man is old enough,
for what you'll behold,
but you'll have to pay for the show,
because nothing in life is free,
and there will be no refund,
once exposed the merchandise,
or the client too excited,
and like the one in Hiroshima,
explodes and dies."
I swallowed deep and said:
"Tarry a while for a year,
my heart is really weak,
and if you begin to show,
what I think you want me to see,
I may go too far,
and in front of your beautiful eyes.

like a bomb from World War II
I may suddenly explode,
and in all directions, fly,
then drop like a rock
and I'll virtually die."

She laughed long and hard,
Before she finally said,
"It's an invitation to have a look,
your screen is large,
but it is hardly big enough,
to be a double bed,
so, what I'll do instead,
is to take one piece at a time,
you'll watch me very closely,
and I will watch your heart,
when it begins to boil,
and uncontrollably shake,
I'll immediately stop,
and you can have a break."

«What if not,» I said,
«or the coming was quick,
or the warning was too late?»
She smiled and then she said:
«If I'm not quick enough,
and you alive no more,
I'll grab my bra,
run out screaming,
and behind me shut the door.
I'll delete your name,
once removed from Messenger,
they tell us, you were never born.»

DOWN WITH OPEN EYES

Down with staring eyes you look,
And up I look at you,
The sweaty parts of our bodies,
Are stuck with lovers' glue,
Sweetest boy with a heart of gold,
Half my thoughts are fears and doubts,
And the other half is you.
Be patient for soon I hope,
I will love you too.

STRANGE SENSATION

I don't know when,
I don't know how,
Just moments after we met,
I felt a strange sensation,
Like that of a gentle pierce,
By a wandering magical dart,
I reached fast for my chest,
And softly, softly pressed,
Closed my eyes and then I looked,
The lock was there no more,
All the lights were on,
To reveal an opened door,
And deep, deep, deep inside,
I found you in my heart,
You moved to make a space,
Waved your hand for me to come,
And sit by your side.

WHY SO FAR?

Why so far,
My little star,
Why so far?
It's worse for the heart to fail its pace,
Than to see the joy is gone,
And home to sadness is your face,
I asked you then and I ask myself,
My little star,
Why so far
You withdraw
When you have me next to you?
Why retreat?
When you know that you and I,
Have exactly the same heartbeat,

You leave a shadow behind,
I looked; it's not mine,
It's a shape I neither love,
Nor I understand,
So, stay with me,
We can both withdraw,
And we can both retreat,
But both of us will always know,
If we have to reach for a hand,
It will be yours or mine,
We'll be together,
If we are,
Don't worry,
You and I will be fine.

THE EYES OF ME

For a while now,
I have been awed,
By a pair of eyes,
No soul is there,
To see,
No heart, no mercy,
And not a touch of care.

They're just two eyes,
No blink is there,
No depth,
It is just a stare.

Who could it be?
I ask myself again.
With courage I asked:
«Who are you?»
«Don't worry; it's only me.»
«Who's me?» I asked.
A shrug was the answer.
«You are scaring me; who are you?»
Another shrug followed by:
«Go to a mirror;
look at it and you will see.»

KALI KALI ZULFON

Kali kali zulfon ke phande na,
Hia la tathkor wa ana la ansa,
So, tell me gods who never rest,
Why am I doomed to remember,
And she's free to forget?
My love is far too great,
But my heart is far too small,
We know you are forgiving,
And we know you love us all,
But can't you ask the sun,
To burn her with my love,
Or only if she loves me,
The moon agrees to shine,
Or else if not possible,
Make us both forget all,
Or order both in love to fall?

Kali kali zulfon ke phande na,
Listen to the warning,
And young men beware,
To love and be unloved,
Is the greatest nightmare,
And like life itself,
Love is not fair,
If all lovers go to hell,
The loved ones will not care,
Guards are their shadows,
And jealous is the air,
Like the old charmer,
Who turned men to stone,
Promised all who look,
To love them all alone.

Black, black are the eyes,
And dark black the hair,
One shoots magic arrows,
And the other burning flare,
The hearts are the target,
And the chests totally bare,
You shouldn't have looked,
You did and now trapped,
And for the rest of your life,
You'll live in despair,

Kali kali zulfon ke phande na,
Why can't I forget,
And why can't she remember,
Hear me all who want to love,
For the sake of God Ga,
Save your innocent souls,
And learn from my affaire,
Unrequited your love will be,
By girls with black eyes,
They want you to see,
But shield your eyes quickly,
And promptly leave the ground,
Never look back but if you dare,
You will be trapped,
You may look around,
But safety from black eyes,
You will find nowhere.

This poem is dedicated to the memory of Ustad Nusrat Fateh Ali Khan, the king of qawwali.

WOMEN AND WINE

Don't ask me why,
I love you so,
But tell me that I must,
You need me there when you cry,
And there when you lust,
Have courage and walk in,
My heart is an open gate,
I'm for you and you're for me,
And our love is our fate.

Don't ask me why I love you,
But tell why I should,
If I know I'll let you know,
But only if I could.

Women and wine can be divine,
But only when they wait,
If the love is right
And the time is right
Early is too early
And late is too late,

PAIN KILLER FOR LOVE

Can there be love without pain,
Can there be spring without winter,
Can there be seas without rain,
It may be the pain of love,
Not for the one you now have,
But the pain that will await you,
If forced to love again.
Years and years of second attempts,
May happily pass,
Then things begin to change,
Likes for likes or more for less,
It could be a flash of memory,
Many tastes of a single kiss,
Suddenly you may realise,
The real love of your life,
Is someone else.

First is first in love and life,
The second is always next.
But hold her closer to your heart,
She's the painkiller of your first,

Love and time do heal,
One day you may realise,
The love of your life,
Is the one you have,
And great it is not small,
For the one you loved before,
There was a door,
But now it is just a wall.

SHINING GIRLS

Forget the brain,
And go for girls who shine,
No man is known to have ever,
Proposed to Einstein.
Forget the looks,
And go for a man with a heart,
Whatever you do,
He'll stick with you.
The handsome man,
Will make a call, or two,
Then nail in bed,
Your best friend,
And behind your back,
When you are out,
And inside your own flat,
Once on bed and twice on a mat,
Unashamedly he'll do,
Your loving sister too.

YOU ASK ME IF I LOVE YOU

You ask me if I love you,
I ask you if you do,
I know you wish you didn't,
And you know I think so too,
Lovers will not be lovers,
Unless every morning,
They fall in love anew.

YOU SAY YOU LOVE ME

You say you love me,
Can you tell me why,
Am I the pearly light of your moon,
The brightest sunshine of your day,
Am I gentle, cute and fair,
Am I the things you may tell me,
And the things you wouldn't dare.

You're good at seeing through me,
If I say it, it's a claim,
I am a woman, and that's true,
But true is not the truth,
And both are not the same,
But you can make them one,
With words I understand,
Tell me I always give you,
Peace of heart and peace of mind,
Or else just hold me,
And whisper loud that you'll love me,
And always, always will be mine,
And every time you think of a reason,
If I hear it will be fine,
And you will be rewarded each time,
In a different way than the one before,
A new one I will try,
With images and with sound,
But you have to close,
All the windows and the doors,
And just in case,
Keep earplugs at hand.

WHO SAID I'M GOING AWAY?

Sweetest heart,
Don't cry,
Who said I'm going away,
To Hell or even Heaven,
When I finally die?
Half of you is mine,
The other is your dad's,
From your mum one eye,
From dad the other,
Wherever you go,
Whatever you do,
Whichever you see,
Both of us,
Every single second of time,
Are always with you.
When you cry,
Touch your tears,
So you may feel,
They are mine too,
We are thrilled you're alive,
Because both of us are living,
In you,
Look in the mirror,
And see my face,
Together we go,
To every place,
So why the tears, my sweetest,
Why?
If you really love us so,
Why do you want us to cry?

FORGET TOMORROWS

Forget tomorrows,
And let your minutes last,
A present lost,
Is a future with no past.
Forget your pains,
Your failures and regret,
We can remember all of them,
But also, can forget,
Disappointments too,
And wounds of heart and mind,
Steel yourself,
If the cure is not within,
It won't be found outside.
And fear not another love,
Another try, and, yes, indeed,
Another rejection or a scorn,
A cactus fruit will yield its sweet,
Along with a stinging thorn,
Give and take, measure for measure,
And seek them out,
The others are not the enemy,
The enemy is the other,
They are where the pain may lie,
But also, where the pleasure.

GOOD MORNING WORLD

It's breakfast time,
Toasted bread, a fried egg,
A cup of coffee,
And on top of all,
Garnished with a smile.
Which should I savour first?
The heart asked the mind.
It's from a girl,
Like all girls,
Whole or in part,
Hard to understand,
But only for the mind,
So, step aside and let me say,
That girls have the habit,
Of treading softly,
And more softly dart,
Like the soft wind,
Of early spring,
With no barriers whatsoever,
All the way to the heart.

Good morning world!
You can have it all,
But leave me her smile,
If only for a while,
Until it is engraved,
Deep inside my soul,
She has a key,
I can't remember gave,
I had one,
Now there are two,
It was supposed to be a secret,

But they find out,
Girls always do,
And a boy can't hide,
She is in his heart,
Her loyal spy inside.

LIFE WITHOUT A WOMAN

Life without a woman is possible,
No bickering and no fuss,
But drier it is,
Than the driest desert,
And utterly, utterly pointless.
So go ahead scream and fight,
There's no day without a night,
And when peace reigns again,
And off is turned the light,
Whichever women you will hold,
She will be all right.

WHO HUNTS THE HUNTER?

It was said,
By the nation of Ād,
That the might,
Of the All-Mighty God,
Not in the strongest,
Will to be found,
But in the weakest,
Of the kind,
That's why the ancients said,
Men are taken,
Girls are won,
That's the rule,
Under the sun,
In the past it was this way,
And it's true even today.

All the creatures,
In the land,
Are either hunters or preys,
All is won by the hunter,
All is lost by the prey,
Humans are the perfect hunters,
But they don't behave this way,
Boys are always chasing girls,
To get them where they want to play,
But soon the hunter will realise,
That though he did all the chasing,
All the time the girl was hunter,
And all the time the boy a prey,
Stunned by her stunning eyes,
And captured by a dazzling sway,

Handcuffed for ever and ever,
By a love of lasting spring,
A promise for both to keep forever,
Witnessed by a wedding ring.

I SAW YOUR SMILE

I saw your smile
But didn't see
If it said "let us be"
Or "what will be will be".

As you know, it's not a train
If when missed it will return
With regret there will be pain
But people do move on again.

Meeting eyes are not a glance
It's an invitation by chance
Join in and love somebody
Or watch life behind a glass.

For the twining to complete
Boys and girls have first to meet
Every heart has a secret key
Waiting for lovers to find
That's why when we kiss
We close our eyes
In the hope that we may see.

MY LOVER IS A WALL

Is this what's all about;
Love, I mean?
One minute,
I'm the richest girl in sight,
The next, my love account,
Is absolutely clean?

Speak to me!
What wrong did I do?
Be it large or be it small,
We already have,
Four of them,
Do we really need,
A fifth wall?

My body still aches,
From a desire with no end,
I can't sit down,
And I can't stand,
But I do understand,
I didn't make you a coffee,
And that's true,
But for God's sake,
Give me a break,
Go ahead,
And make us two,
One for me and one for you,
At least you can stand!

You want to be a wall?
Fine; you'll have your deal,
I'm also a wall,
And I'm all sealed,

No sex for you,
No meal,
No yes for you,
No deal,
Until you come around,
Or go back to your old lover,
Before we met,
And love your hand.

NEXT TIME WE MEET

Next time we meet,
Be it day or be it night,
Bring along whatever you want,
But keep away your doubt,
A headache is a headache,
A cut is cut,
A stomach upset is a stomach upset,
But doubt is a voracious disease,
Grow and grow it will,
And it will endure,
Don't infect me with it,
It doesn't have a cure,
So open your heart and listen to me:
Of love, my heart is made,
And here I am as open as can be,
Look at me as deep as you'll see,
Then hear him out,
My heart would like to say,
My love, my life, my agony and my bliss,
I'd rather have you for a day,
Then all my life with someone else.

SEX IS A SERIOUS BUSINESS

Listen boys and listen girls!
For what I say is best,
First is first,
And seconds are always next,
Seconds are seconds,
And thirds are always late.
If you must play with dirt,
Make sure it's washable,
Whims are sins in every case,
When forgiveness is impossible.

It is said revenge is a plate,
That's best eaten cold,
If that's so,
Wives' revenge against husbands,
Should wait until they are old.

If you can't handle the shove,
Don't push people around,
Tidal waves are more destructive,
Than earthquakes underground.

Kneel before your wronged woman,
And ask her for forgiveness,
It's one kneel, you silly boy,
But after that,
Her kneeling will be endless.

It's neither gentle nor cruel,
To say otherwise is nonsense,
Most girls will understand,
That sex is a serious business,

It's a game for boys and girls,
And both will do some gifting,
The girls will loudly cheer,
And the boys will endear.

HIGH TOWERS

I can see the future,
So all of you are warned,
You may want to stay,
Or choose to run away,
But there is no escape,
Better stand still,
And hear me if you will,
False is the system,
And criminal is a design,
For all of us to be in debt,
Then people in high towers,
Will force us by law to repay,
Most of us will not be able,
For their money they'll own us all,
And the world as we know it,
Will stagger and finally fall,
And thrives are the plagues,
A few are the money masters,
And most of us the slaves.

TIT FOR TAT

My eyes are wet,
My heart is dry,
Dark is the day,
And unanswered is the "why"?
Wave after wave of drifting worries,
Are mixed with resident pain,
A scented message they send to you,
Trying to reach your shore,
Look into your eyes and ask you,
Please, please, please, please,
Talk to me and tell me why?
The tide is there,
Low and high,
And I don't know,
Why my message would return,
I'm told there was no recipient,
The house has no door,
No windows and no light,
Another try was even worse,
«Undelivered» they told me,
The shore was there no more.

If I reach for you,
You should reach for me,
And somewhere in the middle,
Both of us will be,
One-sided love,
Is not the love I want,
And only when your Eros yells,
You are nice to me,
Not only joy is shared with you,

But pain is shared too,
If not there when needed,
Come your turn to need me,
And I will not be there,

Blame me all you want,
But in this case,
A tit for tat is fair.
I'm better with you,
I can tell you that,
And I need a shoulder,
When I cry,
Be kind to me,
If you're not,
I'm better without.

FOOLISH THOUGHT CALLED LOVE

Now that the scene is set,
And rushing fears with rushing tears are met,
With a distant voice you look away and say:
From wall to wall you filled me whole with love,
In every way and every part you touch,
I'm always aching everywhere, I swear,
If this is a crush, I'm beyond repair,
But that's not all,
There're things you do and things you say,
Can make me dare or hide away,
And blush.

I can't remember,
No, I can't remember when I last said no,
If that's so,
Why do I sometimes feel,
I love you far too little,
And sometimes far too much,
And why do I feel still,
Sometimes I'm in heaven,
And sometimes deep in hell?
And with a text away or just a naughty call,
Will be together rolled close to a ball,
My body is burning but the soul is cold,
Lonely and scared the dizzying height of love,
Could turn around in a flash,
And freely begins its fall.

Don't get me wrong, I am strong.
Whatever happens our love will endure,
You make me laugh and you make feel secure,
It's a foolish heart, I hear you say,

I know,
But what's love if not a foolish thought,
If not to dare and not to stare,
And not to dance unaware
Of all else but two loving eyes
That softly whisper in your ear: I care.
If hearts can dance, they would be on the floor,
Their left is right and less for them is more,
They may appear the source of joy,
But don't be fooled - it's pain they enjoy.

AM I A BLOODY BITCH?

Am I?
Perhaps I am,
It just happens,
That if you have a bloody lover,
You may have a bloody bitch,
Confused and confusing,
You start afresh,
And after an hour or two,
You become like him,
Confused and confusing,
And no more you will know,
Who is who,
And which is which,
And who's bitchy,
And who's bitch.

Please let me tell you this:
My love for you isn't a dream,
It's not a whim,
it's not a sexy steam,
It's as solid as steel,
And sharper than a blade,
It's the stuff of strong hearts,
From which love is made.

It may be time for a fresh start,
Or may be time to part,
And both decide for both of us,
Who is who and which is best,
It all depends if we're ready,
For each to press the heart,

Take a breath,
And together will count:
One, two, three,
Reset!

WAITING HAND

I'll take your waiting hand,
And pressed against my lips,
I'll count the reasons why,
If both of us are lovers,
And both of us are loved,
If both of us are honest,
And both of us are true,
If both of us may take
A bit less than we give,
If both of us may talk,
A bit more than we do,
Things will be fine,
As long as we live,
Don't let the myths worry you,
For soon you'll find,
That heaven and hell,
Are only in our mind,
The one that's real is Earth,
Our home and that of our children,
Only we can make it hell,
Or else make it heaven.

LOVE IS COURAGE

Love is courage,
Love is fair,
Kiss me if you want me,
Hug me if you care,
Let me nestle in your arms,
Not just in your dream,
And if you are true,
I will love you too,
I'll take you in my heart,
And as you'll care for me,
I will care for you,
And when I see your love for me,
Sparkling in your eyes,
It will be the time for me,
To whisper in your ear,
Love is courage,
Love is fair,
Take me if you really want me,
And love me if you dare.

I AM THE ONE FOR YOU

With every beat,
In every vein,
With every take of air I breathe,
In every way you want me,
And every way I can,
You will be loved,
You will be mine,
Again, again and again,
Until the end of time,
But I'm not a dream,
Come the morn I'll disappear,
I'll be around,
And I'll be here,
For you and for me,
To tend to what is dear,
No compromise,
My precious prize,
If you remain the one for me,
I am the one for you.

BURN THE SKIES WITH FLAMES OF MAN

Burn the skies with flames of man,
And torch the wind with wonder,
We were made of cosmic dust,
The diamond powder of thunder,
We are the creators of gods,
In our temples they wander,
Of hanging gardens in the sky,
Of pyramids reaching for the stars,
Of dreams beyond and yonder,
We are here to change the world,
Not sent down for a blunder,
When time comes to say goodbye,
Send us back with a joyful cry,
Not with a tearful whimper.

A PLACE IN MY HEART

Don't worry when we part,
You are with me all the time,
No matter where you may go,
You shall always be with me,
Because I have you in my heart.

ONE MORE DAY OF LOVE

Is there a way?
Is there a way to make you stay?
Is there anything I can do?
Is there anything I can say?
I'll walk on my hands a mile,
For half a smile,
With my lips I'll hold your tears,
Before they stream,
Wipe the sadness off your face,
Look deep in your eyes,
And tell you again, again and again,
You've been always my dream,
And then tell myself and you,
There is nothing I won't do,
I'll even defy myself,
Go to a temple,
Kneel below a pile of stones,
And pray,
And all this,
And all the more you want,
Whatever it is,
Just to let me love you,
One more day.

THE GIRL FROM ALBANIA

She is Albanian,
With vineyard grew and olive trees,
Green meadows and fresh breeze,
Combined with all of these,
The wish of all the fairies,
To be the fairest of the fair,
And the country's best envoy,
Her many admirers swear,
Not just because she's refreshing,
And not just because she is a girl,
In everything, some will tell you,
She is uniquely one of a kind,
Astonishing her positive energy,
A thousand girls just like her,
Would turn our world around.

You'd know girls by the way they walk,
Who is happy and who is not,
Whose eyes are always searching,
And whose eyes are always shut,
Who is anxious for a twine,
And every twenty-two thousand,
A shy virgin would pass you by,
She's not looking for attention,
And she is aware of what she is,
A vaquita species of humans,
On the verge of extinction,
By boyish hordes of Neanderthals.

In different parts all girls attract,
But She was created differently,
Watch her walk and you will see,
The attraction of all the parts,

She doesn't walk - she slides,
As if her mother gave birth to her,
On the carpet of Arabian nights.

Some men can't stop themselves,
One of them is called Andres;
One night she suddenly screamed:
Did you see what he just did?
We shouted: we did indeed,
What a vulgar and distasteful deed;
He walked by and very discreetly,
But unlike the serpent of mother Eve,
Andres lures with his hand,
He stealthily knelt and craftly aimed,
And without a sliver of shame,
Swiftly poked her behind,
And only because Albania is peaceful,
Bombing Colombia was declined.

Hail to thee Albanian girl,
The kindest girl you'll ever find,
And topping her beautiful body,
An equally beautiful mind,
Even when upset she's happy,
And when she's happy we all are,
A smile is a feature she can't hide,
And I'm told by those who know her,
Even when her sleep is deep,
Her sweet smile is not asleep,
Troubles are no longer troubling,
And sadness no longer sad,
For all of us lucky to know her,
She'll always be one of a kind,
And truly she is to all of us,
One of the pleasant gifts of God.

THE SPRING OF LOVE

The spring of love,
Is always short,
Its days are always numbered,
Like a candle in the wind,
After a word or a look,
Love may suddenly glow,
And burn with desire,
Then all of a sudden,
A mysterious whim will blow,
And bring to an end its fire,
No more warmth,
No more light,
No more life,
No more hopes,
Life that thrived with love,
Is nothing more than a corpse.
Love is a dream with eyes closed,
And a dream with eyes opened,
But nothing lasts forever,
And all will come to an end.

A SEA OF TEARS

Gloom was crushing,
She had no will to be,
Her tears dried,
And she could hardly see,
She would if she could,
Her life for a lost child,
Is cheap,
But the hopes are shallow,
And the fears far too deep,
For her and mums before,
It was time to weep,
And weep she would,
Until a sea of tears,
Will stand,
Where once she stood,
It's waves mauled by fears,
And the depth is mixed with blood.

Take care of little ones,
And protect them all the time,
Each of them will die just once,
And for whom all will weep,
But broken hearts of dads and mums,
Each night will pray,
Soak their eyes with tears to sleep,
And wake up dead the next day.

THE HARDEST PRISONS OF ALL

Oryx eyes between Rasafa and Bridge,
Wafted towards me love from corners I know,
And every corner I don't,
To which girl my love should I pledge,
For friends, sweet for me is love,
And bitter is love for me,
Is there a way to have the sweet,
And let the bitter be?
To a friend I heard her say: lose him not,
Feed him with your love,
So he may stay,
In portions large and small,
And listen to what I say:
There isn't a power more potent to sway,
A prisoner of love,
Is in the hardest prisons of all. *

A translation by Adel of parts of a poem by Ali ibn al-Jahm (803-863 AD).

RESTLESS SHADOWS

Gentle is the night,
Bright is the moon,
Two hearts in a trance,
Beating in tune.

Restless are the shadows,
Anxious is the air,
It's a call for love,
Answer if you dare.

Reluctant are the blinks,
Constant is the stare,
What heavens created you,
My most enchanting girl?

I've answered the call,
She now has them all,
In one hand my heart,
In the other my soul.

Stand please,
All of you,
For here she comes,
My girl amazing,
My breath you took,
What a wonderful sight,
When you turn to look.

OF ALL THE GIRLS I LOVED

I wish that all lovers,
Who died for love,
And all lovers,
Who felt its pain,
To come at night,
And meet my girl,
To tell them all,
What real love,
Is all about.

When both can give,
Then both can take,
When both are free,
And both are one,
When one is cold,
And one is a flame,
When made are mistakes,
And both take the blame,
When tempers are changing,
And kindness is the same.

Of all the girls I loved,
You're the one,
The only one,
And after a lifetime of love,
And very few days of pain,
Our youth will be gone,
But young our love will remain.

HAPPY WIVES

An iceberg burning, I have seen,
An elephant inside a hive,
A star swallowed by a baleen,
A man suckling at ninety-five,
A farmer ridden by a donkey,
A pile of wood being burnt alive,
But never, never in all my life,
Have I seen a happy wife,
But etymologists appear to believe,
The last one may have been Eve,
He couldn't have loved another woman,
Aside from her there were none.
It is like so one is told,
Things today unlike before,
The handsome man she married,
Is unrecognisably old,
His face is an image deformed,
Of jovial youth obliterated,
His biting teeth and shiny hair,
Are either fake or there no more,
And even the pubes are bald,
Kissing is messy and sex a bother,
And like old tea with no sugar,
A long time ago the burning love,
That warmed them both is freezing cold.

Don't laugh,
Both of you are young,
And both of you are bold,
But close your eyes for just a second,
Open them again,
Then look:
Horrified you discover,
Both of you are old.

You are innocent victims,
And old age is guilty,
We shouldn't be alive at ninety,
Soon we are unfit,
And one or the other will quit,
Time is not still,
And one day they'll wake up,
And forget both they will,
For years they slept head-to-head,
And now they'll begin to scream:
Who are the two bloody strangers,
In my bloody bed?

SLASH

The greatest pain,
You can endure,
Is an abandoned heart,
An innocent love severed in a flash,
Will have no cure,
And time may leave you with a scar,
More painful than the slash.

WITH OR WITHOUT YOU

Close your eyes.
And tell me what you see,
Is there a life out there,
Or a life is yet to be?
Is there a tomorrow,
Or tomorrow is your past,
Life is going quickly,
And death is chasing fast,

Is there a girl out there,
Waiting for a twine,
Or do you think two are many,
And lonely will be fine?
If you do,
I have a word for you:
It is better with,
But with or without you,
Girls will be loved,
And on life will go,

SOFT SKIN

Soft skin and softer touch,
Beckon the eyes to close,
And in the midst of a wild dream,
A pause,
Suppose my darling, just suppose,
I tell you now, "I love you,"
Would you say, "We'll have to see,"
Or, "Why so long it took you?"
And would you want me to be true,
All my life to me and you,
Or would you think,
That just like a rose,
Love blooms,
Then gets tired of time,
Pulls a cover over its eyes,
Swallows deep,
And dies?

A THOUSAND YEARS OF LOVE

Of all the girls I loved,
You're the one,
Who touched my troubling thoughts,
And now they're gone.

Of all the girls I loved,
You're the one,
Who cured my fear of love,
And now it's fun.

Of all the girls I loved,
You are the one,
Who taught me how to love,
And now it's done.

Is there a way,
For me to repay,
Your kindness and your love?
You know I do,
I pray to you,
But is there more?
I wish my heart can be,
A revolving door,
Each time you pass through,
I'd love you more,
I wish that you'll have
A thousand happy lives,
Free of worry and pain,
In each of them, and all of them,
You will remain,
The dream of all my dreams,
The glory of all glories,
The girl I want to love,
Again, again and again.

MUSLIM GIRLS

Prayer time is prayer time,
And other times are fun,
Heart and body for the one we wed,
Not like others for everyone,
We are mares born to race,
We don't need a test run,
We will walk and you can watch,
But keep a distance and don't touch.

Some of us will wear a veil,
So the jerks can be stopped,
But if we see a man we like,
Accidentally will be dropped.

Casual sex is not for us,
Free samples we don't send,
But know you must our sex appeal,
Can drive Deepika[1] round the bend.

Ram is Ram,
But "ghazal" and "Leila" in Islam,
We've invented the word "Ishq",
And from Islam 'salam',
The one we love "ashiqui",
And if he makes us dizzy with love:
"Habibi", "hayati", "nassibi".

We do fast in Ramadan,
It's a month for all to pray,
After that just name your game,
However naughty we'll play.

---

[1] *A sweet Indian actress.*

If you are a Muslim boy,
And you can say Subhanallah,
We will say Mashallah,
So don't be shy to stop and ask,
We'll say 'yes' if you're right,
After that you'll have to wait,
The snacks you miss in patience time,
Will be waiting on a plate,
Big or small, snipped or not,
Are always welcome every night.

So don't call us names,
And spread your lies,
Malice and insults too,
Circumcision is not for us,
But if somehow you will persist,
We're Muslim girls, so watch out,
An eye for an eye and a tit for tat,
The only one to circumcise,
Is you!

NANNY AND GRANDAD

Nanny and grandad,
Sometimes can be fun,
Albeit rare,
Just like a London Sun,
Last Sunday we woke up,
To howls from Nanny's room,
To the rescue rushed,
My dearest loving mum,
And out she came,
Laughing all the time,
Apparently, she said,
Your nanny and your grandad,
Six months to the day,
Managed to have some sex,
With what they have for plumbing,
The pleasure, however, is slow,
And only today at break of dawn,
They suddenly realised,
That with speed they were coming.

That minute was medicine time,
For hearty nanny to take,
When she heard what mum had said,
She shrivelled like a prune,
Coughed so hard,
And harder swallowed,
And like a circus acrobat,
Out flew the medicine,
And in went the spoon.

Nanny's vengeance was swift,
Mum's story dried her pride,
So she'll flood the kitchen,
She filled a balloon with liquid soap,
And hid it in a bundle,
When my mum was not looking,
She put it in the washing machine,
Closed the door and turned it on,
Then called her cat,
And marched in distinction.

She stopped and listened,
From the cat there was no sound,
It was nowhere to be seen,
But seen was the bundle,
And she could hear the machine humming,
Looking through the glass door,
In horror was mesmerised,
As the cat was freely spinning.

EVERYTHING I WANT TO SAY

Everything I want to say,
A thousand times was said,
But there remains a few,
I'll whisper in your ears,
When we are in bed,
Now I'll wait a while,
It's all up to you,
But I'll say 'adieu',
If it isn't "I do".
Once said I am willing to wait,
As long as you want to.

BEDTIME STORY

Dearest mum,
I love you,
I really do,
And I have a question,
For you,
I can see,
That our daily bread,
Is brought by my dad,
A gift to you and me,
But they say it's from God,
Is that true?
And mum,
My lovely, lovely, mum,
When I'm sacred,
I come to you,
And you and dad will hold me tight,
And safe I feel again,
All through the night,
And early in the morning,
With a ticklish kiss,
You wake me up to go to school,
And before I leave,
Another kiss,
And "God Bless",
But then they say,
It's God who keeps me safe,
Wakes me up.
And lets me go to sleep,
Is it true?
You love me so,
And always hold me dear,
Not Hell and Heavens,

Are mums,
Just love,
Love with no fear,
And whatever I do,
I know deep inside,
You won't burn me alive,
Or smite me with your sword,
Just because once or twice,
I acted really bad,
Or friends in class I told,
I love the mum I always find,
Not the god I don't.
My lovely, lovely mum,
I know,
You don't want me to,
But if you do,
I'll happily worship you,
And I'll be glad,
To let the horrible boys,
Worship a male,
Boys' only God.

MAKE ME HAPPY

I know you say:
"I try",
But try some more,
It shouldn't be that hard,
Like the letters of the mail,
One day they make me happy,
And one day they make me sad,
Not too much,
Just some more,
So you'll be the one,
Who wakes up,
With a smile on his face,
And you'll be the one,
Who swims in my dreams,
When I go to sleep,
Not the one,
Who makes me shine one day,
And one day,
He makes me weep.

JUST FOR ME

Is there a way to your heart,
Just for me,
Or wait I must,
And you shall see?
I breathe the smell of honey,
But I only see the bee,
The song of the old wandering hearts,
Many times has been sung,
Give me a sign,
You'll be mine,
Cause I really think that you should know,
I am ready to be stung,
And I don't mind if I wait,
Like a nightless day,
Or a moonless night,
As long as the wave I want,
Is coming back,
And won't return with the tide,
And leave me alone,
Alone, alone, all alone behind.
If you tell me I must wait,
And again and again wait I must,
Because once I said that I love you,
I will tell you in your face,
Again, again and again,
I am a liar and I lied.

WHAT GODS CREATED WOMEN?

You are created by what Gods?
In which part of Heaven,
It must have been ten or twelve,
It couldn't be just seven?
Of what essence you have been made,
Was it the purest cosmic dust,
Was it the sparks of God's lust,
Was it the work of all the moons,
Jealous of its brightest shine,
They wanted the Sun to fade?
It is true what has been said,
That the Gods first created woman,
And to the woman they gave their bless,
And after a life of admiration,
They created everything else?
Shine on us, you beautiful women,
The brightest stars we've ever seen,
Give us love and give us hope,
Each of you is a perfect angel,
Each of you a perfect lover,
Each of you a perfect mother
And each of you is a perfect queen.

THE SHRILL OF LOVE

Of course, I'll shrill,
What else is there to do,
When you charge,
With the fury of a drill,
What you boys don't understand,
Is that we are alike and different,
We both sigh,
But don't ask me why,
You have nipples,
What for I've no clue,
And wouldn't tell you if I knew,
But you are not a girl,
And just like you,
Sometimes I'm stupid,
And sometimes I'm sane,
Sex is not only pleasure,
It is also a killer of pain,
Of course, I do,
I love you,
But I'm not alone,
My body too,
Must join in,
And only then,
I will belong to you,
And you belong to me,
That's what we were,
And that's what we are,
And that's how it will be,
But you have to be gentle,
We women scream of joy,
And we scream of pain,
You should know which is which,

I don't know,
Like a solider in a battlefield,
I'm busy pushing back
Thrust after thrust,
With no shield.

RAMEEN

There is a girl in Pakistan,
Fresh as a daisy in the fields,
Pretty as the moon in full bloom
Kind with a heart that beats with love,
And a soul so pure,
It is like the pure water
Of the river of Heaven,
She is the Eastern star,
Of the world,
And like her,
She has a beautiful name:
Rameen,
Let all lovers stand for her,
And in one voice full of admiration,
Shout,
Rameen! May you live long and happy,
Amen.

THE STRINGS OF MY HEART

I don't have a violin,
For the tune before we part,
Instead, my music shall be played,
By the strings of my heart,
The only joys eternal,
Are those of women and men,
Strangers shall they meet,
To become the closest kin,
To bind is not a sin,
The sin is not to bind,
We before all things living,
Must surely understand,
Of course, I will,
And wait and hope,
For you I'll still,
But let's be clear.
The dearest for a loving heart,
Of everything that's dear,
Life is short and youth is even shorter,
If not ready take your time,
But no need to pretend,
Worse than "I'm sorry,"
Is waiting with no end.

THE PRICE OF TRUTH

Is the price of truth,
An assassin from hell,
A mutilated body,
An orphaned child, friends,
And the few prepared to tell?
Is the price of silence,
For a promise not to tell,
A multi-zero check,
And a hot cappuccino.
At a villa on the hill?
Can we ask those who don't,
And those who pray,
Do we honestly know,
In the maze of modern jungles,
Who exactly is the predator,
Sent to kill a lonely prey?
Outside the city of peace,
The ancient cross is there no more,
A new one has been raised,
Prayers in words and tears were said,
Now in silence the people wait,
The full price next to God,
By a brave prophet of truth,
Already has been paid.

Daphne Caruana Galizia: We won't forget.

BONDS OF LOVE

If bonds of love,
are made above,
is true,
then why resist,
I have the best,
the only man,
I want to love,
Is you.

I should with care,
deal with an affair,
so, new,
but what the heck,
you make me tick,
the only man,
who makes me dare,
Is you.

At times, before,
I had a doubt,
or two,
but when once more,
after your kiss,
instead of no,
I whispered yes,
I knew.

I knew that love will come one day,
And take my doubts and fears away,
I never thought it'll be so soon,
There was no music, dance or moon,
I couldn't even find any words to say.
And when you took me in your arms,

And love twinkled in your eyes,
I knew you love me like I do,
How did you make me fall for you?
I never planned for it this way.
But if bonds of love,
Are made above,
Is true,
Why the wait,
I took the bait,
I want to take,
Your hand one day,
And gaze at you,
See my love in your eyes,
and softly say,
I do.

WHY DO YOU WANT MY HAND?

We are girls and we are clever,
And we are dying to be loved,
Not just for a fluidal night,
But for a full year of light.
However, the other day a man came,
To ask for my hand,
Surprised, I said to him: I need my hand,
How else can I pick my nose or poo,
If I give it to you?
I am a girl, and that's true,
But I know that men use their hands,
For what girls are supposed to do;
Your hand for what you need looks fine;
And unless two you have down,
Why on Earth do you want mine?

WHAT CAN I DO?

What can I do,
To make you change your mind,
And put your doubts to rest?
Is it all right to call,
Or maybe wait is best?

Is there a way,
To make you hear my sighs,
As longing as can be?
Or should I be content,
With a sad sigh just for me?

Is there a way,
To make you close my eyes,
For a daily dream to see?
Or should I pout my lips,
And *will* a soft breeze,
To take my kiss to you,
And bring your kiss to me?

What should I do?
I do love you,
And out of heart,
I want it out,
For the entire world to see,
It will take a while,
And come what may,
I WILL love you,
You WILL love me.
But you won't tell me,
So don't tell me,
Say it to your heart.

One day I'll find a way,
Your heart and mine will take a walk,
Under a tree he'll kiss my hand,
And he will finally say,
What you can't.

VINEGAR AND WINE

All the hours of all the days,
And all the minutes in between,
By all the Gods I'll swear to you,
Again and again I'll love you,
But if one day,
After a kiss,
In a moment primed with wonder,
You sigh deep and then you say,
Sweeter than the sweetest wine,
Your lips,
I will remind you, yet again,
The grapes milked for their wine,
Are also milked for vinegar.

MY DEAR

Summer is dead,
And autumn young forlorn,
Winter cold will be bold,
Gathering all the storms,
And fast convulsing,
Demanding to be born.
Very soon it will,
Nothing can stop it,
Life will be struggling hard,
And before long it will be still,
A new season has just begun,
And old seasons died.

It is a season of life and death,
Of drying souls that had enough,
Of arid fields that yearn,
For new meadows beyond time,
Measured in seconds and years,
By spirits dull,
And maidens looking for loved ones,
But they see none,
The days are dark,
And the nights are full of fears,
Their hearts are crushed,
And their eyes full of tears.

Life needs death,
As much as death needs life,
Tears are water soiled by grief,
Preserved long by salt,
It's bitter,
But life is bitter and our blood,

Will testify to that,
A strange liquid mix,
Of salt, sugar and fat.
Rain will bless life,
New or resurrected,
The embryos wait for spring,
And their souls again will bring,
Hearts as well,
And life.

Don't worry, my dear,
Your body is old,
But your spirit is young,
Wait for a while,
Until I steady my soul,
And don't worry, my dear,
If we make it through winter,
We'll make it through the year.

THE MIRACLES OF LOVE

All fairy tales are fairy tales,
And a dream is just a dream,
Come morning light they'll fade,
Like raindrops in a stream,
But miracles all the time are made,
With a sudden glow,
That shoots across the sky,
And underneath you will see it -
Two lovers who just confessed,
Hand in hand are passing by.

HANDCUFFED BY A RING

It was said,
By the ancient nation of Ād,
That the might,
Of the Almighty God,
Not in the strongest,
Will to be found,
But in the weakest,
Of the kind,
That' why the ancients said,
Men are taken,
Girls are won,
That's the rule,
Under the sun,
In the past it was this way,
And it's true even today.

All the creatures,
In the land,
Are either wanting or wanted,
All is won by the brave,
All is lost by the slave,
Those with the bravest heart,
Will knock on the girl's door,
Then say:
I want to love you,
Please show me the way,
And don't close your heart,
I'll knock on it every day,
If you like poetry,
I am a poet,
If you want jokes,
I know them all,

If you want me to jump,
Ask all my friends,
And they'll tell you:
I am a Kangaroo,
If you want me to kiss your hand,
I'll gladly do,
If you want a star,
I'll climb all night,
And get you one,
Give me your heart,
I swear you won't regret,
I'll love you like no man,
Ever loved before,
Here is my hand,
Handcuff me to you,
You have no sword,
You have no knife,
But a pair of snaring eyes,
And a most beautiful smile,
Like that of a goddess,
And shining like the ring,
You'll wear,
The moment you say "yes".

A FAIRY TALE

House to house,
And door to door,
The oldest wandering singer,
Beneath a wandering moon,
With the last bleeding finger,
Strikes a bleeding tune,
Away with shame,
And fear no more,
Not every man a Satan,
And not every man a saint,
Not every woman an angel,
Or the devil's incarnate,
But when both are joined,
A door in Heaven is opened,
A rose of love,
Out of the rocks of time,
Opens up and blooms,
With a glowing look of scorn,
The ugly death is eyed,
And challenged by the bold,
And every time a child is born,
A fairy tale is told.

SIT WITH ME AND CRY

Come sit with me,
And I'll cry no more,
They're not the tears of sadness,
And not the tears of joy,
But don't ask me what for,
My memory is blurred,
And my mind confused,
Tears are pure,
When they flow,
The heart is washed,
And the eyes and heart can see,
Far too many things in our lives,
Are not supposed to be,
Men and women in masks,
Demand to be seen,
And praised for lovely smiles,
And very beautiful eyes,
But they are deformed,
The nose is below the lips,
And the eyes vertical,
The other disgusting features mix,
Beauty surgeons looked,
And all shook their heads,
"We can't do it," they said,
"They are horrid, and even God can't fix."
The good things have aged,
And the bad are all what's left.
Medicine can be poison,
And tears my only cure,
I've told you some of the reasons,
And others were told before,
So, sit me,

Hug me long and cry,
And I'll cry no more,
Just sit with me,
And think how disappointing we can be,
And the terms we now hear,
"God is dead," they say,
"And money is bread,"
"Down with love," they shout,
"And long live the sex,"
Heaven is a city of whores,
And Hell is a bank,
And blessed is the kindness of the cruel.
All is pointless, scum and dirt,
"Yes?" you must say,
But neither "no" nor "why",
So, sit with me,
Count my tears and cry,
They are not mine,
They are God's,
And I heard him say,
"I thought I created Earth and Heaven,"
"How come Heaven now is hell,
And Earth is the farm of the wealthy,
The meek were promised to inherit Earth,
But they poor and hungry,
And all the deeds were sold,
All the rich are ugly,
And the beauty queens are bald.
So, sit with me,
Tears are truth; they never lie,
Hug me close, then kiss me,
But I won't hug you back,
Until you kiss away my fears,
And share with me your tears.

TO LOVE AND SUFFER

To love and suffer is far better,
Than being happy without,
No place on Earth is emptier,
Than a loveless, empty heart,
Sometimes love is heaven,
Sometimes love is hell,
Sometimes love is tears,
Sometimes joy as well,
So sweep away your tears,
Your foolish doubts and fears,
And shine with a smile,
When you do,
If only for a while,
I'll take your anxious hand,
And pressed against my lips,
I'll count the reasons why,
If both of us are lovers,
And both of us are loved,
If both of us are honest,
And both of us are true,
If both of us may take
Bit less than we give,
If both of us forgive,
Forget and reset,
IL, the glorious He in Heaven,
To us will be kind,
For doubts and fears are only,
Temporary residents in our mind.

Listen girls, all of you are precious,
And you're stronger than you think,
So trust IL; don't be afraid,

Times happy will come,
And sweet words are said,
Hearts will be moved,
And promises will be made,
With every beat,
In every vein,
With every breath,
For every day,
And every way men can,
You will be cherished,
You will be loved,
Ug's face will darken,
IL's face will shine,
All of you are his daughters,
All of you are blessed,
And each and every one of you,
Will be loved and all will be fine.

BROKEN HEARTS

Every end has a beginning,
And every beginning has an end,
Stand tall when occasions call,
And bend when you have to bend,
Broken branches and lonely stems,
Were stubborn trees that defied the wind,
But in matters of heart think again,
Always, always think again,
Hearts are not bastions,
They are difficult to defend,
Broken hearts are not hearts broken,
But broken women and men.

I WANT TO FALL IN LOVE

With a sudden rush for seats,
The train was almost full,
And next to me is a girl,
Listening with a great thrill:
"... and love," her mum went on,
"Is right for old and young,
But only if they have chocolate,
And they're good to their mums,
And they are pure and faithful,
And always pledge to be true.
The angel of hearts is in a castle,
With a large enchanting hall,
Those he invites to dance,
He'll send in a magical thrall,
And before his song is over,
Singles are joined in pairs."
I want to spread my wings,
And fly like a homing dove,
To tell the angel of hearts,
I'm ready to fall in love,
I've always loved my mum,
I think she's an angel too,
I have his favourite chocolate,
And I'll always be true.
I've believed in him,
Since I was a little girl,
One day I'll tell my boy,
Waiting for me out there,
Come take my heart, it's yours,
I have been waiting too,
But now that I'm ready to be loved,
The angel, I was told, lives nowhere.

WHATEVER THE BET I'LL PLAY

What should I do,
So you'll believe,
My love is true?

What should I say,
Except the truth,
The snow is white,
The grass is green,
The sky is blue,
And I love you.

If it's naughty you prefer,
I'm as naughty as you'll get,
Just name your game,
Tell me when and tell where,
Whatever the bet,
I'll play.

If serenity is your taste,
I am fine,
Calmer than the calmest sea,
I'll tiptoe in and tiptoe out,
And only when you feel your lips,
You'll know the warmth,
That lingers there,
Is mine.

There's a key to every lock,
And to everywhere a way,
I have a heart,
And I also have pride,
It could be yes,

It could be no,
And neither has a mask,
When 'yes!' is your answer,
I'll ask.

COME BE MY CHRISTMAS

Come be my Christmas,
And I will be New Year,
Every day of every week,
Year after year.

Join me in a new beginning,
To put an end to fears,
Water sweet my drying soul,
And I will dry your tears.

Like the time and like the tide,
Lovers are free and lovers are tied,
Show me that you'll always love me,
And hide what you need to hide,

Love stories told and told,
Of lovers young and lovers bold,
They'll never weaken; never be old
If their love is their child.

Come be my Christmas,
And I will be New Year,
I shall always love you,
Year after year.

A NOVEL READ BACKWARDS

Every different time we meet,
I have the same question,
Just after "hello",
And just before "goodbye",
Of all the girls around,
"Why did you choose me?"
I ask you again and again,
But alas, all in vain,
You don't tell me why,
And I don't have a clue,
Whose fault is that?
Only two to blame?
Either me or you.
Please understand,
We've never met,
We've never kissed,
We've never been in bed,
And I have never held your hand,
But you know too much about me,
Were we lovers in another life?
Or will be in the future?
If so, it didn't last,
And if so, you need a rupture,
That takes us either to heaven,
Or sends us deep in hell,
Either way I have my doubt,
Sometimes I feel troubled,
And you need to tell me fast.

He nodded and stepped aside,
"I have a novel I'd like you to read,
After that we shall meet,
Either no more you'll see me,
Or I'll be the one you'll see.

All this is very strange,
How come I lived in a country,
Never before I've seen,
And to have fallen in love with you,
Never more astonished I have been,
But you are right I'm she,
As for you I'm not really sure,
You seem to have left me,
But you didn't tell me why,
Was I in danger, or was it you?
But I remember a goodbye kiss,
And I remember I raised myself,
And kissed you too,
And both of us cried.
You smile but it's very shallow,
And there is sorrow on your face,
I know the reasons,
So, I'm not going to ask you why?
But you know very well,
That sorrow always makes me cry,
In time I'll try to love you,
To wash your sorrow but more than that:
Will you love me if I try?
Will you really make me happy?
Or will you really make me sad?
One day you and I will sit,
Never before closer,
And closer still my heart,
It's our lives not the novelist's,
If upset can take a hike,
We'll tear the last few pages,
Push them down his inky throat,
And write the ending that we like.

LIFE FOR MOST OF US

Life for most of us,
Is difficult when at best,
The lives of the few is not,
But soon enough,
And come what may,
They will join the rest,
And in the count of friend and foe,
We may realise one day,
That the price we pay,
For those who betray,
May be nothing compared to those,
We foolishly may trust.
A long time ago we left a jungle,
Of mainly predators or prey,
But look around,
And you may find,
We live in a jungle OK,
Graveyards of broken hearts,
Frail shadows of forced smiles,
Forgotten promises,
And sweet dreams preserved in salt,
And I can see,
I can see the brightest eyes,
Dimmed by the darkest fears,
Overwhelmed by strings of lies,
They drown in running tears.

NO OTHER REASON

Girls will be women,
And boys will be men,
And both will be lovers,
And both will be kin,
Until their hearts can love no more,
Or the cycle turns again.
And girls will be women,
And boys will be men.
....

Does life have a purpose?
Or a journey with no end?
What use is all the answers,
For questions we can't find?
The ancients knew,
And we should too,
The words for "love" and "life"
Are one and the same,
The purpose of life for them,
Was the perpetuation of life,
In our words they seeded,
And no other reason was needed.

WHERE DOES TIME GO?

Where does time go?
I wish I know but I don't,
And how could I answer this,
If time itself doesn't know?

What is different for him and me,
Is that I'm a being and he is *BE*,
If both of us will go somewhere,
We'll only know when we are there,
Meanwhile it would be nice,
For all of us to have a clue,
Hell, or heaven are both all right,
At least we know where we are,
But what if neither is true,
And the truth is far too far,
The worst of all is to live again,
Knowing, as we all know,
A thousand hours of happiness,
Do not equal an hour of pain,
happiness is a memory we can't feel,
And soon forgotten but pain is real,
It is like a desert eternal,
And not a drop of rain,
Seek not the gods for happiness,
Happiness does not have a god,
Only we, make others happy,
And only we, make others sad.

YOU KNOW BY NOW

You know by now I'm many,
And not one is like the other,
But don't let that worry you,
A garden is not a garden,
If the bloom in one flower,
Nor rainbows are rainbows,
If they have a single colour,
So, look inside,
And choose the one you like,
But love all of me,
Or else let me be,
We are two and one,
And though one will love you,
We also love each other.

THE WAITING GAME

He was always early,
She was always late,
The kiss for the time watcher,
The heart for those who wait,
A myth is told and retold,
Of the hunter boy and the hunted girl,
The truth is known and truly old,
The girl is always hunter,
The boy is always bait.
Some may call it a waiting game,
Others prefer to call it fate.

WE WILL BE FINE

We'll give and take,
And grateful for luck we will be,
If it doesn't come our way,
Our luck we can make,
I have no doubt,
Come what may,
With your resolve and mine,
We'll do what we can,
And as long as we are together,
Whatever life throws at us,
We will be fine.

KINGS AND QUEENS

In words not so sweet,
Twice you have told me,
That for your taste,
I don't have enough meat,
But you already know,
Where it matters, I do,
And not just that,
Whatever you want,
I want it too,
And I only ask of you,
To love me before and after,
And treat me like a queen,
If you do you will be king,
And I'll love you before and after,
And the time in between.

THE CAPPUCCINO GIRL

The heart was heavy,
And the mood was light,
When at Delicata late at night,
A drink favoured in heaven,
On Earth was to be made,
A warm, creamy cappuccino,
Topped by a floating heart,
Guested by a sweet mermaid,
What words can be added,
When all the words are said,
By a single smile of «thank you»,
Returned by angelic eyes,
And «enjoy it» by the head?

Flow as you come,
And flow as you go,
The old poet told the boy,
Who didn't seem to know,
You are looking at a garden,
And all the roses girls,
Concealed is desire,
But burns inside like fire,
The steps are hesitant,
And the passion gasping fast,
The one who dares will win,
And those who fear are last,
In a place parents and lovers meet,
Heat their wills and cool their feet,
Why look above for angels,
When angels real are here,
For the boy dazed with beauty,
Any of the girls is fine,
And come what may, he promised,
One of them is mine.

It took some time to twine,
And on a Christmas card he drew,
A heart inside a cage,
And just outside a question mark,
She dropped her head,
And looked at the floor,
Then wiped a tear and looked at him,
Like she never did before,
"I couldn't wait for you to say,
What in silence I have said,
A thousand times and more,
As long as you love me,
You'll be the one I adore."

HOMO FORNICATOUS

Once I was a scholar,
But I don't remember where,
Maybe it was Oxford,
Before it was there,
I'm famous for my theory,
On the purpose of our lives,
Some say it is explosive,
Others it is rather flat,
In simple terms,
I told my cat,
Without being rude,
It's good to wear clothes,
But better in the nude,
As all Homo fornicatous,
The skinniest and the fatous,
Are either busy bonking,
Or else getting bonked.

SORROW

Which door should I knock on,
To get you to reply?
What answer would I get,
If I ask you why?
What would it take,
To have your love back,
Or tell me what to do,
To stop an anguished pain,
The first one almost killed me,
Do you want to kill me again?

You feel sorrow for me,
But 'sorrow' is not 'sorry',
And it is 'sorry' I need,
If you want me to be.

Every time you cross my mind,
I fold my arms around my chest,
And hard, hard I squeeze,
For fear my heart will break away,
To rest in your hand.

Soul, listen please,
You are wiser than my heart,
So please tell me,
Is my heart beating for me,
Or for her beating too,
And I know no more,
If it belongs to me,
Or if it belongs to her.
You may choose to do nothing,
And wait for me to beg,

That I wouldn't do,
Once only I'll say «please»,
And then no more,
And believe me when I say,
Everything that will happen,
Has happened to me before,
There will be a different girl,
And there will be a different door.

YOU CAN'T FORGET

To forgive you have to forget,
To forget you have to remember,
The bitterness of things forgotten,
Will suddenly become alive,
And alive with them regret,
You realise you have been wronged,
People think they can change,
But they can't and will wrong again,
Next time is another time,
Your tolerance will be ignored,
And greater will be the pain.
You shouldn't have remembered,
But allow the memories to fade,
They'll be alive for a long time,
And a high price will be paid,
And now you can't forget,
Therefore, you can't forgive,
The only thing for you to do,
Be it a friend or be it a foe,
And be it a husband or a wife,
Is permanently slam your door,
And eject them out of your life.

THE PRICE OF SUCCESS

Don't fear the price of failure,
The price of success you should fear,
Only if you do you fail,
If you don't, you'll never do,
You've given all your best,
But success for some,
For others a failure,
And that they can't accept,
Agitation becomes the norm,
A threat after a threat,
Turmoil is now your life,
And there isn't the time to rest,
You see anger in their eyes,
And you feel it in what is fed,
Truth is slaughtered by the lies,
And easy to destroy than build,
The aim of all should be clear,
Little men and jealous women,
Will crush everything that's dear,
In time you will realise,
Not all enemies are the same,
The distant ones will use sticks,
The closest the longest knives,
After years and years of love,
One day fears will wake you up,
You are healthy but somehow ill,
You have heard what was said,
And the actions are louder still,
You turn around and shake your head,
You didn't know and now you don't,

Who is ugly and who is not,
Who is leading and who is led,
And who in hell crept at night,
Lying next you in bed?

There's no sweetness in vengeance,
If never there was a crime,
Time can heal but surely not,
Poisoned is the heart of time,
"Don't' be sad," little Vicky chimed,
I will always be your friend,
I will kiss you every morning,
And I will hug you every night,
Both of us will be happy,
And everything will be all right.

AM I IN LOVE WITH A SPOON?

Something I'd like to tell you,
Before I must forget,
I have loved for far too long,
And it's time for me to quit,
More rewarding to love a spoon,
Than to love a poetry twit;
Some poets are not so bad,
But most of them are shit,
He dedicated a poem to me,
But it's about someone else,
"What's the difference,"
He would say,
Both of you are equally loved,
And both of you were in the way,
When we were in a single bed.
This is the rubbish I always hear,
That neither please nor endear,
With him I 'll never know,
At what point should I be coming,
But always know when I should go,
No apologies and no remorse,
And I wish to God we were married,
The happiest day of all my life,
When I file for a divorce.

The mind of a poet is a meat-grinder,
Where truths and lies can easily mix,
A creative mind is a twisted mind,
And that's a problem God can't fix,
He has the dream of a little boy,
To live on top of a mountain,
The highest ever can be,

But that's a dream for one,
I have a dream for two,
I see something he can't see,
One day soon he'll know for sure,
The greatest dream he'll ever have,
Is me.
If he shuts up all is well,
To the man I love I'll come running,
And the spoon can go to hell.

I AM A BANKRUPT HUSBAND,

I am a bankrupt husband,
And I weep when boys tell me,
How much they pay for sex,
My wife is far more expensive,
And her VAT is sixty six,
You'd think it's enough; not so,
I must pay for every kiss,
Entry and exit fees,
And generous gratuities and tips,
No wonder then,
Before I married a millionaire,
Now just a thousandier,
Or less,
An afterthought is this:
Hugs are totally free,
And nil is VAT,
But only if she's out,
And I am alone with her lingerie.

THE GREATEST KILLER

Life and death are eternally twined;
Along with the contract of life,
The contract of death is signed,
We are born weak,
And weak one day we'll be,
The unknown rages out there,
With a face we'll never see,
Blame all you like,
But death is not guilty,
And dying is not a crime,
All of us are innocent victims,
And the greatest killer of all time,
Is time,
Where did it come from?
Where is it going?
Does it have the chaotic moods of girls?
Or the impatience of little men,
What power drives it?
We don't know,
But maybe, like everything else,
If it had a beginning,
One day will have an end,
A new moon,
A new Sun,
A new world will be born,
We don't know what lies ahead,
So, instead let all of us pray and hope,
Raise our arms all their length,
And tell all the gods,
When all assessments are done,
You gave joy but death and sadness too,
Give us now a happier one.

THUS SPOKE ZIRYAB (1)

To be careful with the heart is wise,
To fall in love is wiser,
Having loved and failed is hard,
Not to have loved is harder.

Seek forgiveness from yourself,
For your sins young and old,
Others won't let you forget,
And neither those you told.

If you wait for bad things,
Bad things will come to you,
Good things are the same,
If called they'll come too.

They are a book with a single page,
And near the middle a single line,
Girls Will Be Girls
All the prophets tried and failed,
And all the gods can't change.

There's something in your fist,
You'll do anything to defend,
One day you'll open your hand,
And find nothing but wind.

True strength is in your soul,
Strength from others has a cost,
The least help you're likely to get,
Is from those you helped the most.

Every girl is a princess,
And every man a man,
Only a gentle woman,
Can make a gentleman.

All girls are born angels,
Let's keep them so if we can,
But if one becomes a Satan,
Be fair and blame the man.

Go ahead and speak your mind,
And don't worry about refute,
Our voice is there to be heard,
And silence for the mute.

Listen to me all Libras!
Not every man is for himself,
But afraid to fail all others,
One day you'll fail yourself.

Steel yourself and meet your end,
You've taken and now you're giving,
Hell is not eternal death,
Hell is eternal living.

Lonelier than any human,
Is the god who sits above,
No friends, no family, no sex,
And neither lovers nor love.

There's a trick for those in love,
Covering body and heart,
The longer the kiss with closed eyes,
The sooner the legs will part.

New lovers should be patient,
Only birds in cages sing,
If she doesn't have her winter,
He's unlikely to have a spring.

To fall in love man must see,
For a woman she must hear,
The gate to the heart is his eye,
For a woman it's her ear.

Men's anger is a passing noise,
Women's fury will sustain,
By the time the fury is over,
Almost nothing will remain.

Women hate when men are late,
The waiting is always painful,
But a speedy coming is even worse,
When it is time to be playful.

Love is love and sex is sex,
Decide the best and take it,
A good advice is to go for love,
As hearts will never fake it.

Like an empty bottle of perfume,
Only the memory is yours to keep,
The burning passion of old lovers,
Is to lie down and sleep.

Lips will dry if lonely,
But they glow if kissed,
Singles lead a wasted life,
And couples will be blessed.

What's good for gander husband,
Is good for wife goose,
If the boxer is loosened,
The G-String will be loose.

Boats and women are anchored,
Usually side by side,
Two weeks of labour are needed,
For a 20-minute ride.

Sex for women is not a meal,
That they'll have to bake it,
But a cold meal is not rewarded,
And that's why they fake it.

If life and death at a certain time,
Should make you feel pensive,
Life lived at any price,
May be too expensive.

The parting of two lovers,
Is always, always sad,
But nothing spoils a love story,
Than a marriage going bad.

Love to the full or not at all,
It's either this or the other,
No one is loved like a child,
And no one loves like a mother.

Mistake you learn from,
Can be a fair price,
Learning from mistakes of others,
Is far quicker and nice.

Our life does,
But time doesn't fly,
Unnoticed when living,
And unnoticed when we die.

A foolish man would be worried,
If every brain is out,
A wise man should be worried,
When every fool is right.

Of all things plurally,
Nothing is harder to build,
And nothing is easier to break,
Than the backbone of a family.

Wounds of the heart may heal,
Just like any other wound,
But unlike all other scares,
Their pain will never end.

Pinnacles are conquered,
Because youth is always bold,
The wisdom of "I told you so,"
Is the wisdom of the old.

Protect the innocence of your girl,
And safeguard her wonder,
The grapes that make the wine,
Are the grapes that make the vinegar.

HUG ME AND LET ME CLOSE MY EYES

Hug me and let me close my eyes,
One breath I feel and then no more,
I see a garden of roses,
Invite me to come inside,
I look around and around,
But a door I can't find,
My tears are screaming,
And silent is my heart,
Which door is yours to knock?
When will you be kind again?
It was a mistake, I confess,
But I paid for it with my pain,
When again will you love me?
And for how long should I wait?
I am a woman,
And I know what to do,
With or without your help,
I will make you love me,
I'll do this for me,
And I'll do it for you,
And you will not resist,
So don't raise your fist,
Soon you'll thank me,
You and I know,
A loveless heart,
Is an empty heart,
It might as well not exist,
Our love is not made for us,
But the one together we can make,
I know you have moods,
So we'll need it to be strong,
And neither I nor you can ever break.

SOMETIMES

At a certain point in our lives,
Late or later will realise,
The very little that we may have,
Is all what we have,
And it needs to be protected.
But what is there to protect?
Life is fair but we are not,
Most of all to ourselves,
Conned we are of a beautiful dream,
Hiding an ugly nightmare,
Whatever we do,
The little will be little,
And the helpless will not help,
The gifting will be bare,
The weak will have no strength,
And the careless will not care,
Wake up and look around,
The soft mud we stand on,
Is not a safe ground.

It's hard to explain,
Why some of us will flower,
And some of us will pale,
And why few of us will make it,
But most of us will fail,
Life is not a mother,
But an epical violent river,
Impossible to reign,
Dredged are the rootless,
And the anchored will remain.
Believe in God if you wish,
And believe in others if you dare,

Only the strength within you,
Will force the fate to be fair,
To trust most others,
Is to trust in despair.

LOVERS MUST LOVE EVERY DAY

Love has a face seen in mirrors,
With misted eyes through a dream,
Its colours will dim by fears and errors,
And the shadows won't be what they seem,
Birds of love are always restless,
Their wings are arched ready to fly,
We can guess more or less,
But who knows what the reasons are,
It may be because no one loves like another,
And no two hearts are the same,
It could be her; it could be him,
But no one really is to blame,
Lovers dream with eyes open,
And think with mind closed,
Love is earned not given,
And always with a price to pay,
There are times to remember,
And there are times to forget,
No matter how long will live,
Very short is love's memory,
To keep it safe from regret,
Lovers must love every day.

MEN ARE DOOMED TO LOVE WOMEN

You were a source of pleasure,
Now a source of pain,
A cold swim then a colder shower,
And a migraine after a migraine,
What remedies to cure desire?
When the flames will not be still,
Can you extinguish fire with fire?
When desire burns like Hell?

Of all the arsenal Eve can wield,
Desire will have no shield,
Give up, men,
Millions tried before you,
You hear them shouting,
In the graves:
"Men are doomed to love women,
All of them will be defeated,
And none will ever win,
Look at me and look at him,
We are definitely dead,
But still think of them,
And even some almighty gods,
During the day are infallible,
And during the night will sin."
But think of it in another way,
If all women will go to Hell,
Because they are the source of sin,
Only the stupid men,
Would want to go to Heaven,
I am married and I will advise,
If Heaven is all what you want,
Whatever your woman says,
Seal with "Amen".

THE JOY OF LOVE

Wouldn't be great,
Wouldn't be divine,
If all of us will fall in love,
Before it's too late.

And wouldn't be fun,
If everything I have to do,
To make you love me forever,
And make me love you all the time,
Is done.

Wouldn't it be sweet,
If we do part,
We will remain closer still,
And every day we meet.

Wouldn't be glorious if the stars,
And all the moons above,
After the longest kiss,
Whistle long in admiration,
And begin to rain on all of us,
The confetti of truest love.

Immediately after a drink,
Let's hold hands,
And happily sing:
Mornings are not mornings,
Without a morning kiss,
And nights are not nights,
If each other we miss,
Love is the joy of life,
And the joy of life is us,

Let's ask all the gods,
To bless all loved ones,
And make us all lovers,
And as soon as we can,
With the help of all who care,
Make us all dads,
And make us all mothers.

SELVI SADO

Selvi Sado with one 'o',
This is to say to you "hello",
And thanks for giving life to this book,
And making a dream come true,
Believe you me when I say,
It would have been quite impossible,
To build, rebuild and create,
Without a co-author like you,
And now you can have a rest,
And I'll do that too,
And stop lecturing a veteran author,
On what he shouldn't,
And mustn't do,
The beauty of co-authoring,
Should be clear to all,
As each can blame the other,
Be it big or be it small,
For one or all mistakes,
Thanks also for the flying kiss,
You launched at me a century ago,
I checked again for it,
And they told me it's on the way,
And it will be definitely received,
The day after no other day,
Remembered always that moment,
When I saw you very clearly,
As if it was today,
Under a naked sky,
Stripped of its cloudy gown,
Tall and proud you stood,
Like Christ the redeemer of Brazil,
Ten miles and six inches away.